Journey

A MOTHER'S ACCOUNT OF LOVE,

LOSS AND SPIRITUAL HEALING

Mitzi Montague-Bauer

with Journey Montague-Bauer

ISBN: 978-1-944027-50-6 (ebook)
ISBN: 978-1-944027-52-0 (softback)

Published by Networlding Publishing
networlding.com

This book is dedicated to my mother
Evelyn June Montague.

She taught me that love is always the answer,
regardless of the question.

Introduction

The following pages were written in the months following my son, Journey's death. Consequently, you will witness my own "dark night of the soul" as I struggled to come to terms with the ever-changing topography of my life. As I watched Journey's brilliant, sensitive and witty mind weave in and out of the landscape known as mental illness I questioned everything I thought I knew about health and spirituality. Life as I knew it collapsed, but there was growth and illumination on the other side. This story is not only about love and loss, it is also about healing, hope and transformation.

Most of my adult life, I felt confident in my approach to health and wellness. I resonated with Hippocrates' statement about letting food be our medicine. My husband Rex and I grew a large organic garden long before "organic" was in vogue. If an illness occurred, I viewed it as an opportunity to seek out any imbalances and rectify them. Occasionally we sought out a traditional doctor, but it was always as a last resort, not a first. To some this may seem contrary or foolish, but to me it simply felt like the most likely way to achieve and sustain health.

An authentic and fulfilling spiritual connection was another cornerstone of wellness in my life, though I found it required more active seeking. I was raised in a home where love was abundant but spiritual teachings of any kind were nonexistent. God was more likely to be used as an expletive than as a reference to a benevolent being.

Like most, I suppose, adulthood brought about questions about my purpose and how my life intersected with the greater scheme of things. I began searching and found a profound sense of spiritual connection in the most unlikely of places; my job. I am a doula, a childbirth companion, which has provided me with the privilege of attending over 500 births. In addition to assisting women through this profound transition in their lives, I have had the physical and spiritual honor of holding hundreds of newborn babies.

What does holding newborns have to do with spirituality? Everything. A newborn baby is the purest form of love there is. They are directly connected to the source of love from which we all come.

Hands down I have felt most whole, most humble

and most in awe when holding my own newborn babies and the hundreds of babies that followed. I began to understand that God and Love are synonymous. If I tuned into the frequency of Love, I felt a response whether I was praying in church, meditating in my home, comforting a newborn or working in my garden.

For me, God, like love, transcends religion and even language. Both are more aptly described as feelings or a sense of knowing rather than something you can put words to. But alas, we still use words to communicate. Therefore, you are likely to hear me refer to God and Love synonymously. I sometimes use Source and God interchangeably along with Infinite Beloved and Creator. You see, to me, they are one and the same.

Countless times during my son's challenges, I prayed to know what the right action was. Often, I would hear the words "be patient" or simply "trust." On one occasion though, I heard, "Make your home within the breath." I rolled my eyes and railed, "What does that *even mean*??!"

Now, a gazillion breaths later, I understand that profound statement to mean this; if we keep our breath flowing freely and consciously while encountering the difficult things in life, we will move through them more quickly and often with unexpected grace.

So, dear reader, if at any time while reading, you

find emotion stirring, I invite you to breathe deeply and know that, as you do, you join me – and countless others – on a path of healing and transformation.

Prologue

Looking up from my writing, I glanced out the window and noticed there was a police cruiser in my driveway; two female officers and a priest were headed up the walk. Confused, I opened the door and invited this unlikely threesome in like they were old friends. Barely inside the door, the first officer asked me if I was Mitzi. I registered that as odd since "Mitzi" is not my legal name. Attorneys, bank tellers and police officers all call me by my legal name, Jeri.

"Well yes, I am Mitzi. But how do you know that name?" I hesitated. "My legal name is Jeri…" Without answering, she asked me if I had a son named Journey. My pulse began to race. I nodded, "Yes, why…?"

"I am sorry, he died this morning. He stepped off the roof of a parking garage."

Chapter 1

When did I fail
When did I stop enjoying
The birds, the trees, the smell of rain
How did I fail
To remember
That now is what matters
That the future doesn't exist yet

~Journey, 2003, 10th grade English

I first became aware of Journey in the spring of 1986, four months before he was conceived. With the warmer months upon us, it was time to shop for clothes for the family since I could now buy winter clothes at a deep discount. In those days, I took discounts seriously, since my husband Rex worked long hours so that I could stay home with our young daughter, Breaha. While looking at men's dress shirts, my mind wondered if I should perhaps check out the maternity clothes. I chided myself. "I still have maternity clothes and besides, I'm not pregnant." Logic didn't seem as influential as it should have been that day. An hour later I emerged from the mall with a shirt for Rex, a Lego set for my seven-year-old stepson Josh, two maternity shirts and some clothes for a newborn.

On the way home, I stopped at the pharmacy to pick up a pregnancy test. In the morning, I was sure that the test would indicate a positive pregnancy, but I was wrong. A few days later I got my period.

As the weeks passed I would catch myself having thoughts like, "We should invest in a new mattress before the baby is born. . ." or "I wonder who I should see for prenatal care since my doctor has moved out of state?" These are weird thoughts to have given the pregnancy test strips had consistently read "not pregnant." Rex and I hadn't talked about another baby, and he was overworked and stressed about making ends meet as it was. I decided to hold off on that discussion.

The following month my period came on time, but I felt pregnant. I was slightly nauseated in the morning, my belly appeared swollen, I could not stand the look, smell or thought of olive oil. It was a regular staple in my diet but had made me nauseated when I was pregnant with Breaha. It is one thing to have pregnancy symptoms when you are pregnant and quite another to feel pregnant and not be. After the third month, I finally decided to talk to Rex about it. I told him that I thought a soul was knocking on the door.

"We either need to conceive a child or tell this one to beat it." I tried to be upbeat about it, but I was serious. "I am tired of feeling pregnant when I am not." Rex looked amused but was noncommittal.

On a sunny Saturday in June, three months after the shopping trip, I asked Rex again what he thought about adding another child to our family. Looking slightly more serious than he had the first time I asked, he agreed to go downstairs to our meditation room, to be still and ask. In the meantime, a friend stopped by to see if Breaha could join her and her children on an outing. I got Breaha packed up and out the door just as Rex came up from downstairs. He had this silly grin on his face and a mischievous look in his eyes. He held out his hand and simply said, "Let's make a baby, Baby!"

Two weeks later when I took a pregnancy test, it confirmed that we had indeed conceived.

Chapter 2

Few things are etched deeper and more permanently in a woman's mind than the birth of her children. The neural pathways are forged not only by the memory of the details, but by the raw, emotional journey she has taken from the first twinge of a contraction to tearfully holding her child to her breast. Although I had the privilege of witnessing the pure love of a child through Joshua, my step son, who always felt like my bonus child, it wasn't until Breaha was born in 1984 that I knew what mothers felt right after giving birth.

Meeting Breaha for the first time, seeing the intelligence and wonder looking back at me through those huge newborn eyes, changed me in an instant. No one ever tells you that, really. Or if they do, you don't truly get it until it happens to you. My heart swelled with joy as I pulled her to my chest thinking, "My baby. This is my baby!" I felt like the luckiest woman in the world.

~

Journey arrived three years later, on the first day of spring, in the warmth and safety of our home. It was March 20, 1987, five days past his due date and my 27th birthday. Birthing at home with midwives was somewhat controversial in the 1980's in Lansing, Michigan, but it felt like the best option for us at the time. It ended up being the best choice because Journey was born exactly two hours after my first contraction. The midwives arrived 20 minutes before he was born. Had we planned a hospital birth, I would have been one of those women you hear about, birthing their baby in the car; their husband driving way too fast thinking he can make it to the hospital, while the mother screams wildly, "Pull the car over. Now!"

The day Journey was born was unusually warm for the first day of spring. The sun shone brightly in a blue sky, and the afternoon temperature reached a balmy 70 degrees. The white lace curtains lifted in the gentle breeze of the open window. It was a wild and surreal two hours, but then, miraculously, I was holding my baby. Still in shock at the wonder of it all, I lifted my son and kissed his wrinkly, wet face. I was overcome with the joy of meeting him. I pulled him close and expected the familiar possessiveness of "my baby!" but instead, I knew with absolute certainty that he did not belong to me. He belonged to the world. For the briefest of moments, I also knew that he would leave me. My mind served up pictures of him traveling the world. Perhaps he would live in a foreign country? Or he would marry, and his wife would become his new family. Those thoughts were fleeting and were soon swept away with the bliss of new motherhood. I simply assumed we had given him the right name and that he would travel the world. That memory faded but didn't disappear completely. Occasionally and randomly throughout Journey's life, I would recall that sensation and wonder.

Whispering words of love and welcome, I dropped into that wordless place of wonder. I inhaled the newness of him; a smell that most new parents know. My midwife friends and I joke that if we could bottle the scent of the newborn, the wars on the planet would cease. Snuggling Journey close, with Rex on one side of me and Breaha on the other, I knew what love was. I marveled that, up until then, I'd had it all wrong. Love is not a verb; it is not something *we do*. Love is a noun. It's *who we are.*

Chapter 3

Journey grew to be a chubby, animated, willful child. As soon as he could talk he seemed to understand wit. He was funny, and we often laughed uproariously at his antics. In addition to his emerging sense of humor, Journey was stubborn beyond belief. I remember wondering how that much determination could exist in such a tiny body. If Breaha was told to do something, she did it when asked. With Journey, he often contemplated his actions first. I could almost hear his mind processing the request and what the odds would be of getting away with not doing it.

We learned, as most parents do, what's a deal breaker and what isn't. For example, as a toddler, Journey did not like to wear shoes or socks. In the summer months, this wasn't a problem. Come December, however, it was a bit of a different story. One chilly Thanksgiving when Journey was two and a half, we showed up at my mom's house for a family gathering. Journey was in a winter coat, but barefoot. His feet were clearly cold, the color of raw meat, but he wasn't complaining. My mom, on the other hand, gave me the hairy eyeball; she didn't understand or agree with this new-fangled way of parenting willful kids. She herself had witnessed this stubbornness but she believed that a child, especially at that age, should just be made to do what the parents tell them to do.

There is something to be said for letting a child learn by natural consequences though, because from that point on, if it was cold outside, Journey donned his socks and boots without a word from any authority other than his own.

~

Building a strong spiritual foundation was as important to us as math and reading. Children however, are so close to the Infinite, that I often felt like they were the clearer teachers in such matters.

One afternoon when Journey was just three years old, he came running from his room where he had been playing quietly with his Duplo blocks. "I am hungry!" and in the same breathless sentence, "Jesus came to play blocks with me!" For several moments, I was speechless. The children heard us pray and refer to God often enough; but Jesus not so much. I had an uncertain relationship with Jesus that came from misunderstandings that took place as a child. Well-meaning family members spent a lot of time trying to convince me, an 8-year old, that I would suffer for eternity if I didn't confess my sins and become saved. So, Jesus and I? Well, we were still working it out.

Breaha broke the silence, "Oh Journey, what did he look like?"

"He was very sparkly," Journey answered with authority. I finally recovered and asked Journey if Jesus spoke to him. "Yes! He said one day I would have a beautiful shiny body like his."

Later that night as I prayed, instead of addressing God, I spoke to Jesus. As humbly as I could, I asked for clarification. "Dear Jesus, why did you visit Journey this afternoon? What does it mean 'he will have a shiny body like yours someday?'" I was hoping for an answer right then and there, but none came. It would be another 22 years before I would understand the profundity of Jesus' visit with Journey that day.

Chapter 4

As a young boy, Journey often said he heard what was going on in other parts of the house while he was asleep. He would report with astounding accuracy that he had indeed "heard" conversations. He appeared to be sound asleep, but some part of him stayed aware of his environment.

I may have dismissed this as childish nonsense if I hadn't had the same experience myself as a three-year-old. My two older sisters needed tonsillectomies and I think the doctor gave my parents a "buy two get one free" deal, because even though I hadn't had any trouble with my tonsils, I ended up being admitted to the local hospital for one too.

I remember vividly being in a crib that looked more like a small cage on wheels. There were several other cages with children in them in this one big room. My mom kissed me goodbye and told me that she was going out for a while, but not to cry, she would "be right back." Although my body slept, I, the consciousness known as Mitzi, stayed awake all night awaiting her return. Periodically throughout the night, and into the wee hours of the morning, I would hear high heels click-clacking down the tiled hallway and look eagerly toward the door. While I could see my small body lying in the bed, I was also aware of the large round clock that hung above the door. I couldn't tell time, but I was aware of the hands sweeping endlessly around the face of the clock.

Finally, morning arrived and so did my mom. I told her that I had been awake all night waiting for her, but she dismissed my story as nonsense or at best, a dream. So when my own son told me he was "awake while sleeping," I tended to believe him.

Another nocturnal oddity in our house was Journey's sleep talking. A child talking in their sleep isn't that unusual; the part that had us scratching our heads was the language that he spoke. I am not a linguist, but I am fairly certain I could detect German, French, Spanish, or Chinese. The words Journey spoke weren't any of those languages; they seemed ancient and he spoke them with familiarity. We could never catch it on a recorder and he didn't remember those dreams in the morning; or if he did, we couldn't cajole it out of him at the breakfast table. This happened a few times when he was four or five and then tapered off. As he grew, the "ancient language" dissipated and his sleep talking included raucous belly laughing, fighting aliens or occasionally the sleepy one or two-word phrase.

As a six-year-old, Journey marveled at the similarities between the solar system and our atomic structure. He would ask me how to spell words like "molecule" or "atmosphere" while dutifully copying the letters with a chunky crayon. He would often inquire about abstract things like "how does this seed know it's supposed to grow into a pumpkin and not a tomato?" or "How do cells know how to divide and grow into a person?"

But it wasn't just physics that fascinated him. One morning I awoke to a racket in the kitchen. While the rest of us were still wiping the sleep out of our eyes, Journey had fished a broken blender out of the trash and had all the parts lying out on the floor.

"Journey, what are you doing, honey?" I asked as I made my way through the screwdriver and tiny parts on the floor.

"I am going to make a swamp buggy!" he told me with excited authority. The kid could build a vehicle out of a pile of trash, was fascinated with numbers and atomic particles, but couldn't read the simplest of words.

Maybe you are not the cells inside you, but the

environment in which they live. You are the juice between the cells.

~*Journey*, Spring, 2010

"One more story," he urged. "One more page." Journey loved books and could beg another chapter out of me nine times out of ten. He would bring along whatever book we were currently reading wherever we went. "Now? Just a page or two," he begged if we were stopped in traffic too long or there was a moment's pause in the daily activities. He had a richer vocabulary than many adults I knew. He could carry on an intelligent conversation with whomever he met, but he broke out into a cold sweat whenever he was asked to read. Even the simplest phonetic phrases had him flummoxed.

One day as an eight-year-old, Journey was still struggling with reading. His eyes bright with tears, he stormed away saying that he hated books and I was a stupid teacher.

Homeschooling had seemed like a good idea until then, but Journey's words stung, and I began to wonder if his defensive attack was true. Believing that perhaps he and all the other naysayers were right, I dialed the local elementary school. The impatient and nasal-sounding secretary picked up on the fourth ring. I hung up on her. We would wait out the school year and decide at a less stressful time.

Our patience was rewarded with something I

marvel at to this day. One day Journey was struggling with phonics; working hard to read simple three letter words, and then, just like that, he started reading. And I mean reading. He skipped right over *The Cat and The Hat* and went straight into young adult fiction. Big fat books with complex storylines. The first thing he ever read beyond a few labored words was *The Hobbit* by Tolkien. After that, I was as likely to see him with his nose in a book as anywhere else.

~

My mom and grandma lived 20 minutes outside of Lansing in the small town of Charlotte. Since my grandma was growing older and my mom was single, my mom moved in with her mother to provide support during Grandma's last years. Weekly, the kids and I would pack up a few things and head out there for a sleepover. "The Grandmas" looked forward to our visits and enthusiastically planned meals around our favorite foods.

They lived on a beautiful piece of property of which my grandma had loved every inch. Flowering shrubs and beautiful shade trees dotted the yard between the flower and vegetable gardens. The huge expanse of yard extended to an equally large wooded area that passers-by often mistook for a park. One day the five of us were out in the wooded part of the yard clearing away the underbrush and the twigs that had planted themselves, aspiring to be trees. Journey ran around wielding his "sword," knocking over anything less sturdy than himself. Breaha on the other hand, stood tearful as my mom maneuvered the spade toward the roots of a scrawny Charlie Brown-looking tree that stood about three feet tall. "Grandma, wait! That tree still has green leaves on it! You can't dig it up." Upon closer examination, there were indeed three withering green leaves sprouting from one of the sticks that Breaha insisted was a branch. My mom, with her boot still on top of the shovel, ready to plunge it into the earth, paused. "Honey, this tree can't stay. It won't get enough light…" Tears pooled and then spilled down Breaha's cheeks. Before either one could speak, Journey stepped in. He asked my mom if they could talk in private. "Grandma, do you think maybe you could dig it up later? When we're not here. That way Breaha won't be sad." And then in a whisper, "She's so sensitive about things like that."

Chapter 5

School days passed with equal amounts of bickering and cooperation, laughter and frustration and the occasional ah ha moment. One cool autumn day I was awakened by a cacophony that sounded like wild animals fighting over a kill. I cautiously opened one eye and saw that it was still pitch dark outside. Covering my head with my pillow I took several deep breaths and counted to ten for the first of many times that day. I thought about the cool science experiment that I had planned for the day and knew with certainty that Breaha, and especially Journey, would be wowed by it. Bolstered by my own enthusiasm, I got up and faced the morning.

It was early afternoon before we were ready to start the "school" part of our day. Eagerly, I went about setting out the science equipment and then began asking questions to lead them to a discussion before the cool part. I patiently waited for them to get their water, and then go to the bathroom, and then quit bickering…again. I sat down hard, took an exaggerated breath and told them sternly to be quiet while I counted to ten. (I wasn't really counting. I was beseeching, "Help me get through this day without causing bodily damage to my children…") A few breaths in, my inner voice informed me quite directly to take them to the park. What? Reward them for this behavior? What about the science experiment? I thought for sure I was losing my mind from lack of sleep or from stress. I started over, this time really counting. But just as clearly, as if someone smarter than me was inside my head, I received the same advice. I opened my eyes and saw two pairs of questioning eyes. I surprised us all by asking "Hey guys, want to go to the park?" The looks on their faces was worth the whole day of agony. "Yay! We get to go to the park instead of school!"

I instructed them to go to the kitchen and pack some sandwiches. I sulked a bit, as I packed up the science experiment for another day. Homeschooling was a big endeavor, one that I occasionally felt overwhelmed by. Oftentimes, after the children were in bed, I would spend the evening planning upcoming classes, always seeking to generate interesting lessons. Occasionally, I would find something that was perfect for both kids' interests and development. The science experiment that I was packing up in exchange for "an afternoon at the park" was one of those lessons.

Breaha and Journey were chatting, amiable as church ladies as they neatly packed us a picnic. I noticed with some amusement the hastily wiped countertops and the afterthought of three stalks of celery tossed into the bag.

Driving to Burchfield Park in Holt, I noticed again that the siblings who had just wanted to scratch each other's eyes out were now on perfect behavior.

Arriving at the park, we made our way into the wooded area where we would put down our picnic blanket. Just a few steps into the woods, we all stopped and stared in awe. There were dozens of colored orbs floating about a foot above the ground. These spheres varied in size from four or five inches to maybe a foot in diameter. They were clear and brightly colored like transparent lenses, but in perfect spheres. Most of them were green, but a few were blue and pink as well. I have no idea how long we stood looking at this beautiful spectacle of nature, but Breaha finally broke the silence, "I wonder if the fairies are having a party?"

Both Breaha and Journey had active imaginations. They had a whole slew of imaginary friends and dwellings that were created out of a pile of sheets and clothes pins. Sometimes they insisted that the things they saw were real. "No really, Mom! The birds helped us make that fort!"

Or, "Listen Mom…if you are quiet enough you can hear the grass grow!"

This was something they shared and often invited me to participate in, but alas, I did not see the helpful birds and even though I laid flat on my belly with my ear to the ground I did not hear the grass grow. That day at the park though, I did get to be a part of the magic. For a short moment in time I could see through the veil that often accompanies us right up to puberty. Gradually, as the pace of life quickens, and we grow more accustomed to looking outward than inward, the veil closes, signaling adulthood. Journey, I think, managed to keep one foot inside the veil before it closed.

Gazing in wonder at the balls of light, I began looking for whatever could source such a thing. I wanted an explanation, the science, the reason for what we were observing. I don't know what I thought I would find, but I remember looking for something to explain it. After a few moments of speechless awe, the spheres began to dissipate one by one.

But the magic wasn't over. As we turned our eyes from the wooded area to the river, we noticed that the sun, somewhat low in the western sky, seemed to be growing larger and brighter and then smaller and dimmer. It continued to grow brighter and then dimmer several times as we looked and commented. The sun was flanked on either side by two columns of bright blue light. I had never seen anything like it and said so. Journey was sure the sun liked our admiration and was growing brighter to show off. I admit with some embarrassment now, that I actually listened to my seven-year-old like he knew what he was talking about. I was utterly stumped and had no explanation as to why the setting sun would appear to be pulsing like that. I told them that there was a scientific explanation and that we would find out together what it was. They both looked at me like they did when I admitted to being deaf to the sound of the grass growing.

Eventually Breaha grew bored of the sun and set about making a fairy house, one of her favorite pastimes. She could find the coolest little shapes of wood or stones and fashion them into a fantastical dwelling. If I were a fairy I would have occupied one of her houses for sure.

I lay down on the blanket still wondering about the balls of light. Journey was sitting on the side of the riverbank carrying on a conversation, with whom I did not know. Later, he told us that he was talking to the sun's wife. She appeared to him from the shimmering reflection on the river. She told him that she liked our morning verse about the sun's loving light and that we all had a similar light inside of us. So, there you have it. "We all have a light inside of us," said the sun's wife. Perhaps it was for that one small pearl of wisdom that we were drawn to the park that day.

The drive home was subdued and yet profoundly peaceful. I remember thinking that my measly science experiment paled drastically to that of the Creator.

Chapter 6

Shaking the hair out of his eyes with a motion that had become as familiar to me as the sound of his voice, Journey informed me that he was finished homeschooling. "I love you, Mom, and up until now, you've been a good teacher." His pencil rapped out a striking rhythm on the cereal box in front of him as he continued, "I want to go to public school. I want to know how I am doing in comparison with other kids my age. And I want to play lacrosse. So, when can I go?" His face lifted into a bright and confident smile that lit up the room. I had to admit, the timing seemed perfect. When it takes the teacher twice as long to create the algebra problems than it does for the student to complete them, well then, it's time for a more knowledgeable teacher. Our laughter, Journey's morphing from a boy's to a man's right before my eyes, and mine easy and tinged with relief, filled the space as we slapped an exuberant high-five. Just like that, we hatched a plan. We would finish homeschooling through the eighth grade and then Journey would begin as a freshman at Holt High School in the fall.

~

There were plenty of adjustments for Journey that first year of public school: most of them having to do with breaking into the tightly formed groups of friends that had been together since preschool.

Persistence and humor were two of Journey's strong suits and eventually they paid off for him. He began mentioning names of friends and there was a lightness in his step. An ease washed over his countenance. It replaced the creases of concentration that had played across his face so often during that first semester. Journey was being challenged intellectually, sort of. He did admit to figuring out what was needed to get a 4.0 in his classes and then doing that and nothing more. I rarely saw him do homework but didn't have a leg to stand on since he aced all his classes.

Journey was an interesting study in contradiction: part cool guy and part geek. He wore his thick mass of dark hair on the longer side and chose clothes that were fashionable but didn't give a whit about designer labels or false pretenses. He moved and spoke with confidence but could just as easily swoop up a toddler and tickle them silly. He played the electric guitar, lip syncing to popular music, but also joined the chess club. Most physical endeavors came easily to Journey, his lean body adapting to whatever struck his fancy at the time. He liked to ride his skateboard through the neighborhood like a tough kid but would hastily wipe away a tear as he discussed animal cruelty or the possibility of someone going without food.

I was lying on the couch reading a book, when in the depths of my consciousness I realized that the telephone was ringing. Being so engrossed in my spectacular book, I did not want to answer the telephone. Ring, ring...it did not stop. I stood up in exasperation, "Don't these people have lives?" I said under my breath, as I resentfully headed for the table where the telephone rested. I began to wonder what inspiration this person might have for their incredible persistence. As I put the telephone to my ear, I heard the terrifying sound of my crying sister. In half a second my entire exhausted and annoyed mood changed. The wheels in my head started turning and curiosity and concern almost overwhelmed me. When I regained my senses I asked, "What's wrong? What happened? Are you alright?"

Sobbing hysterically, my sister told me that she had hit a garbage truck with Mom's new car but the damage was not too serious. She then proceeded to tell me that she was unhurt and that she needed to talk to Mom. Mom had been at a birth for her job and had not slept in over 30 hours. Actually, it looked like Mom had been in the wreck! An hour later the tow truck pulled up in front of our house. I thought to myself that my sister must be out of her mind. The car looked like an accordion!

Mom was weepy for a while. I wanted to comfort her, so I told her how sorry I was about her car and all the hassles. She smiled weakly and thanked me. She told me that she was not crying for the car or the hassles. She felt so sad for all the families who had received a similar phone call; the ones whose kids never came home after the accident. I think my mom cried tears for many people that week.

After many disheartening telephone conversations with Waste Management, our insurance company, and the Sheriff's department, life began to mellow out a little. Selfishly, I pondered how unfortunate it was that my sister had totaled a second car the same week I finished Driver's Education. Eventually we found another new Passat for Mom. My sister now has her own car.

Journey, 2003, 10th grade English

One evening I received a phone call from someone who identified herself as Journey's English teacher. Although Journey had finished his freshman year with a 4.0 GPA, I still thought that perhaps that lazy streak had caught up to him. I took a deep breath and politely asked how I could help her. She proceeded in a pleasant voice to tell me that Journey was one of the most refreshing, complex and enjoyable students she had ever encountered. What had we done to "foster such a bright and curious student?" she asked. "I have two young children, myself, and well, I am just wondering what it takes to raise kids who are so interested in learning, and do it with such enthusiasm?"

"Keep them out of public school," my sarcastic side quipped silently, but I knew that was not the appropriate answer. In the end, I told her that Journey had been homeschooled until his freshman year and that he didn't read until he was nine years old.

"The pearl I gleaned from that experience," I explained, "is that, if children are allowed to learn at their own pace, and are given ample opportunity, they will eventually 'get it'." She thanked me again for such a fine contribution to society.

Chapter 7

Way before I was ready, Journey was a high school senior and talked incessantly about going to college. I had to remind him that to go to college he had to actually apply to be admitted to one. He had taken, and aced, a slew of AP classes; he was destined to go to university if he would just get off his butt and fill out the applications. True to nature, Journey waited until the last possible day to get his *one* college application to the University of Michigan in the mail. Driving him to the post office at 10:30PM, he admonished, "Mom, *what is your problem*? Why are you so stressed? *We have until midnight.*"

Rex was the favored parent that year. Journey's and mine was an easy-going relationship; we were comfortable in each other's company, but that year he seemed a bit prickly. It was as if he was creating friction between us, so it would be easier for him to leave.

Understanding this intellectually was marginally comforting, but I still didn't like it. One day he was his easy-going self, joking and laughing easily and including me in lively conversations. The next he would scold me for ruffling his hair or asking him about his personal life. I found myself either wanting to hug him and never let go or kick his butt to the street.

Lacrosse games, friends, parties and prom filled those final days of high school. Eventually Journey received the letter of acceptance to University of Michigan. He rolled his eyes at my apparent relief, but I think that secretly he was relieved, too.

Not only was Journey accepted into the university, he had applied for and received scholarship money as well. It felt like we were in the home stretch of the intense part of parenting. How had we made it this far without the myriad problems many parents face? No drug use that we knew of, or at least that got in the way of performance. Each child had exhibited a healthy but respectable amount of rebellion, but overall, Joshua, Breaha and Journey were all healthy, smart kids heading out into the world to create their own lives. It was frightening and exhilarating at the same time.

~

Finally, the day came to take Journey to college in Ann Arbor. Milling about the lobby of Bursley Hall were anxious-looking kids and even more anxious-looking parents. Suitcases and boxes littered the large reception area. There was a cacophony of excited young voices rising over the sound of their more subdued parents, as students hurried about finding their dorm information and gathering their keys. Looking around, I saw most of the mothers (and some fathers) discreetly wiping their tears, forcing themselves to wear smiles that didn't fit. The students were snappin' and tappin' and ready to run headlong into their new lives, while the parents looked forlorn and stunned that they were at this place of letting go already.

Having cried many tears that year leading up to college, on that autumn day in 2005, I didn't feel inclined to shed a single tear. We got Journey's few things moved into his dorm, we walked around campus for a while, grabbed a bite of dinner and then said our farewells. Admittedly, Ann Arbor is only an hour away, so there was that. Those crying mothers may have been leaving their fledglings half way across the continent for all I knew.

That night before climbing into bed, I found a small sealed envelope on my nightstand. In handwriting that resembled chicken scratching, the inside of the card read, *"Dear Mom, as much as I want to leave, wherever you are will always be home. Love, Journey."* Ah, I knew I had been too smug about the tearful mothers in Bursley Hall that day. I cried myself to sleep that night. It wouldn't be the last time.

Chapter 8

A few weeks into Journey's freshman year it occurred to him that laundry didn't wash itself. He called one day to thank me for the years and years of washing his clothes, preparing his meals and overall loving him and believing in him. "By the way, the next time you come down, could you bring me a couple more packages of socks and boxers?" Clearly, he intended to spend as little time as possible at the dorm laundromat.

Rex and I wasted no time transforming our basement into the den we dreamed about. It was the perfect distraction to the very empty and quiet house. I was also grateful that my career had matured along with my kids, because by then, in addition to my busy doula practice, I also worked part-time at a freestanding birth center. I appreciated having somewhere to be and the idea of being useful was like balm to my aching heart. My aching heart? Well…actually, that is only partially true; my heart fluctuated between missing my children immensely and doing the happy dance. When it wasn't dancing, it was good to have a job that I loved.

That Thanksgiving was the first time Breaha and Journey were home from school and we were excited to show them the newly transformed den; complete with a leather loveseat and a new plasma screen TV. They were happy for us, but rightfully wondered why we waited until they left for college to get a TV that was bigger than a bread box and didn't live in the closet.

It was amazing to witness how much they had matured in such a short time. Their perspectives had broadened, and their ideas were plentiful. One evening as I made my way into the kitchen to start dinner, Journey suggested he and Breaha make dinner for a change. "Mom, why don't you relax? Maybe go read a book. We'll let you know when dinner is ready."

"Wow…thanks guys." I found my book and kicked back in the recliner with a glass of wine. It was a good novel, but I wasn't interested in reading. The clatter of pots and pans, the laughter and the lively conversation was so heartwarming, I just closed my eyes and savored its deliciousness. After a Mexican feast, we spent the evening playing euchre, taking time between hands to reflect on someone's thoughts or laugh at a corny joke. I had a new favorite age of childhood…adulthood.

~

Journey called periodically; less than Breaha, but enough to let us know that he was thriving. He was still waiting for that class or that professor to "wow" him, but he was patient. In the meantime, he would go to classrooms filled with four or five hundred other students that were often taught by the professor's assistant. These things he talked about with a bit of disappointment, but also with confidence that he just hadn't found it yet. In one conversation, he did admit to feeling like he'd been duped. "You know when you hear that a certain school is competitive? I always thought that meant if you got your degree from there, you had a better chance competing for a good job. What it really means is the school and its grading system creates students that compete against each other. If you miss a class and try to get someone to share their notes, you can forget it. It's like you just asked them for the keys to their car."

Journey worked part-time, took on a full work-load and had a few good friends to socialize with, so if the idea of competing against his fellow students continued to bother him, we didn't hear about it.

Chapter 9

One crisp fall day at the beginning of Journey's junior year, my mom and I went down to Ann Arbor to visit him. He seemed like his usual, happy self, except I noticed that he had some fading yellow and green bruises on his face. There was a cut above his eyebrow and an ugly green bruise high on his cheekbone near his temple. Lifting a lock of his hair I gasped "What happened to you?" My heart pounded in my chest as Journey told us about coming home from a party a few weeks earlier and being attacked by several men. He minimized it. Brushed off our questions and concerns, and changed the subject, "I'm hungry for those crab legs you promised. Let's get going to the restaurant." Periodically throughout the meal and afterward shopping at Kohl's, I inquired further.

"Mom, it was no big deal. They only got in a few blows and then I got away."

"Did you know these people that attacked you?" I asked, my voice an octave too high.

"No," he replied around bites of food.

"Did you report this incident to the police?"

"No. Really Mom, back off. I don't want to talk about it anymore." Eventually the incident faded into the background of life. The bruises healed but some part of Journey never did.

That Thanksgiving, we were all invited to Breaha's new apartment in Midland. What would have normally been an easy, light hearted visit was instead dampened by a sense of disquiet, at least in my heart. Journey wasn't himself. It was subtle, but we all noticed something. Josh told us later that he suspected Journey was "on something." Normally vivacious and always a part of the conversation, Journey was distant, pensive. During a card game that he had opted out of, I stole a glance in his direction. He was staring off into space. I got the distinct feeling he wasn't there. Babies and young children often do this, and it is good for their development, but Journey was an active, fully mature adult, and like I said, it was just a bit unsettling. When questioned, he discounted our concerns. He smiled and told us that he was tired, and school was kicking his butt.

Christmas came and went. Journey was happier over that holiday but displayed a weird fascination with posturing. "If you hold your hands like this when you walk, then you will feel more balanced."

Or, "breathing like this will help your digestion." We walked around with our hands "like this" and humored him by practicing different breathing techniques before meals. Journey was always trying something new, or rethinking the norm, so this quirky behavior was only mildly concerning at the time. It was good to see him happy and excited about new things. As he was packing up to go back to school, he asked if he could borrow our juicer. He wanted to do some cleansing; drink more fresh, raw juice. Of course, we loaned him the juicer and were grateful that he still valued good nutrition.

Chapter 10

February 22, 2009 around 10:00 PM (it's weird how some dates are etched in my mind) Journey showed up unannounced. It was spring break of his senior year and he had hitched a ride home. He opened the door and stood there looking so pitiful that I had to choke back tears. I reached for him, but he looked past me and took a step away. I barely recognized my son. He was rail thin, his face hollow; the gaunt expression accentuated by him sucking in his lower lip. He was holding his hands in front of him in a strange posture like someone suffering from severe arthritis. I wanted to say, "Ha ha, you're joking, right?" but I knew he wasn't. My heart began to race, and a lump formed in my throat. Either Journey was tripping on drugs or he was experiencing some form of psychosis.

The young man that had given Journey a ride stood just behind him in the open doorway. I saw the fear in his eyes and knew it mirrored my own. I am certain he wanted to bolt; instead he carefully sat down Journey's backpack and guitar. Remembering his manners, he nodded in my direction, "Ma'am," and then to Journey, "Dude." He backed out the door and was gone. The door closed, and so did a chapter in our lives. The Journey I knew was nowhere to be seen.

Our friends Dennis and Jessica, were visiting from California for the weekend. Not only was Dennis a friend, he was our mentor. I first met him at a workshop when I was pregnant with Journey. I was struck by his wisdom on spiritual matters and moved by his profound love of God. Other like-minded folks were drawn to Dennis' Love and wisdom and eventually we became known as "the fellowship." Whenever Dennis was in Michigan, Rex and I and the kids went to his weekend classes. I was grateful they were visiting because I was so out of sorts and needed a clear perspective. Journey seemed happy to see them and it took some of the awkwardness out of the situation. They came to the door and greeted Journey like nothing was amiss.

"Hey Buddy, how's it going?" And then straight to the point, but without offense, Dennis asked, "Are you tripping on drugs right now?"

Journey assured us he was not. There was an attempt at small talk as Journey brought his things further into the house. This brief pause gave me a moment to breathe and attempt to rein in my fear. It didn't work very well, reining in my fear. My mind was racing, "Should we call an ambulance? Or take him to the Emergency Room?" If he wasn't using drugs, he was clearly having a psychotic episode. Rex and I have several friends trained in mental health, and I am sure any one of them would have told us to get him to a psychiatric hospital as soon as possible. In retrospect, maybe we should have.

Rex suggested that Jess and I go soak in the hot tub or watch a movie, or…anything other than hover around wringing my hands, my eyes shiny with unshed tears. Clearly, my fear wasn't helping the situation. I took their advice and stayed out of the way. I wondered what had happened to my son; the young man who could talk to me openly about whatever was on his mind. Over the past couple of months, that Journey had become more and more distant. Instead of candid conversations, we had stilted, brief encounters. And now, here he was, almost unrecognizable. Eventually the smell of cooking food wafted from the kitchen. I heard forks clinking against plates, the steady cadence of masculine voices, the occasional laugh. I felt the grip in my chest loosen its hold just a bit. The guarded relaxation wouldn't last long.

Much later, after everyone was in bed, Rex and I held each other and cried. We agreed there was nothing we could do that night. We would wait and assess the situation in the morning after some sleep. I soon heard Rex's soft sleeping breath. Try as I might, I could not quiet my mind. I stayed awake that whole night, running "What if?" and "What's wrong?" scenarios through my mind.

The next morning Dennis and Journey were in the bedroom talking. The door was closed. I couldn't hear what was being said, but their voices were low and intense. Then, I heard Journey sobbing. It was heartbreaking, but I was also relieved. The tough guy act was getting him nowhere.

Emerging from that conversation, Journey looked more at peace. He wasn't contorting his face the same way he had been, and he looked me in the eye. He ate small meals. Not much, but more than the nettle tea and occasional glass of carrot juice he had been "eating" for who knows how long.

Again, when asked if he had been using drugs, Journey assured us he wasn't. We shared our concerns and asked him if he felt well enough to return to school. He looked annoyed, "Of course I'm going back to school. Jesus, you guys. What's wrong with you?" Pensive and irritable weren't words I would typically use to describe Journey, but they were the closest I could find at the time. The edginess between us was unfamiliar and I hated it. Since he insisted on going back to school and there were only seven weeks left before he graduated with a degree in economics, we drove him back to Ann Arbor.

Chapter 11

We mustn't be mad at the lot we were given. We must make the best of what we have.

~ Journey, 2010

We were pretty shaken after that spring break incident. Dennis, however, assured us that Journey would be okay. Dennis is an unorthodox teacher to be sure. He teaches that God is in all things, even the things that don't seem "Godlike." He assured me that God had not abandoned Journey, and that Journey was doing the work that he came to do. "Sometimes, we 'sign up' for some tough things in life, but we usually sign up for things that we can pull off."

Pondering what soul in their right mind would "sign up" for this, I recalled Journey's 7th birthday. He and I were downstairs in our meditation room. Apparently, Rex, Josh and Breaha needed to finish festooning the house with balloons or hiding clues to a treasure map for Journey's and my birthday celebration, because we were shooed downstairs and told to wait until we were called.

Some would say sharing a birthday with a close family member is unfortunate, but I loved it. While Breaha was fond of celebrating her birthday on the exact day, even if it was a Tuesday afternoon, Journey, even as a young child, was conscientious about our shared birthday. "You can have a big-people party on our birthday this year, Mom." Journey offered before his fifth birthday. "I will have my Ninja Turtle party another day."

Birthdays at our house were an excuse to spoil the birthday person, or persons in our case, with as much lovin' as possible. In addition to cake, presents, and favorite meals, sometime during the day we would set aside a few moments for reverence; a time of reflection and appreciation. Often this would be everyone present telling the birthday person something that they admired or appreciated about them. On this particular day, the moment arose organically; Journey snuggling close, gazing into the candle light, shared that he remembered seeing the Earth before he was born. "Me and God," Journey said, "we were the same...but not the same, we were deciding where I would be born. From that place," he continued, "everyone looks like a light, not a person.

We are a family for a reason. God doesn't make mistakes." (Okay, so maybe Journey wasn't your average seven-year-old.)

Snuggled together with the world seeming perfect, I smiled and said, "Of course son, God doesn't make mistakes." Thinking of Journey now back at U of M, all I could think was, "Stop! God! I am sure there's been a huge mistake!"

Chapter 12

Our conversations over the next weeks were brief, but Journey assured us he was okay and was looking forward to a bright future. In mid-March Rex and I drove to Ann Arbor to take Journey to dinner and celebrate his 22nd birthday. He seemed happy to see us and was cleanly shaven (what little stubble he had) and dressed in a clean hoodie and jeans.

He wasn't making weird faces, but he did insist that someone keep the conversation going at all times throughout dinner. If he and Rex were eating and couldn't talk, he said I should be talking. Likewise, while I was eating, he or Rex would be sure to keep talking. He patiently explained to us, like we were small children and he the elder, that this was an appropriate tribal ritual. "We've come from a long lineage of people who had to watch their backs. This is how people conducted themselves while eating around the campfire." Rex reminded him that we weren't eating around a fire, but in an upscale restaurant in Ann Arbor. Journey looked at us with… patience…or was it pity? *"Poor Mom and Dad. They can be so simple minded…"*

The food that night smelled delicious, but it tasted like cardboard. My mind was racing. Why all the interest in tribal ritual? Something was going on with Journey and I was frightened for him. There were four weeks before college graduation. Would he be okay until then? In retrospect, I may have done something different, but at the time we opted to wait until he got home in a few weeks to address whatever was going on. To avoid conflict and to support him in eating a healthy meal, we kept up a trivial monologue while we ate.

Despite finishing his senior year, Journey was surprised to discover a devastating blow. Most universities charge by the credit, but University of Michigan charges its students one fee per semester, whether they take one credit or twenty. Friends whose children had gone to U of M warned us that even though their children had been in direct contact with their advisors, the students were told right before graduation that they were missing one or two credits. Journey knew about this potential problem, so he and his advisor had gone over his transcript multiple times to assure he had all the credits needed for his degree. Even though he had been advised that he had enough credits for his degree and took blow-off classes like poetry and theatre that last semester, Journey was blindsided three weeks before graduation. "We are sorry to inform you that you are two credits short. You can walk with your class for graduation, but you will have to take a basic statistics class before you receive your degree in economics."

Journey went back in the fall to take that last class, but he never received his diploma.

His college days ended with little fanfare and even less celebration. He did not want to walk with his graduating class to receive a reproduction of a diploma. He was hard on himself for everything those days. Rex and I bought him a graduation gift that he asked us to return, telling us he hadn't graduated yet.

We helped Journey empty out his apartment in Ann Arbor and moved his few belongings back home for the summer. Three days later, my sister Dawn died unexpectedly. It was a shocking and tragic loss for our family and the beginning of a three-year period where my mom would experience the death of two children and two grandchildren. It was one of those times in life where it was a blessing we had no idea what laid ahead. It was at my sister's memorial that a friend of the family, who had not seen Journey since he was a young boy, asked him who he was. His reply, "I am nobody," was a chilling glimpse into the upcoming hell that awaited us.

Journey's high IQ was paired with an equally high proclivity toward mulishness. After returning home, it was apparent that in his mind we just weren't smart enough to "get it." "You guys I'm okay." Impatiently, he added, "I'm doing a social experiment. Relax."

You may have heard the quote by Oscar Levant, "There is a fine line between genius and insanity"? The second half of that quote is "I have erased this line." I thought that Journey was erasing the line. Even in my most fearful moments, I still believed that he would "come around." Unfortunately, I had the mistaken belief that it was my job, as Journey's mom, to figure out what was needed to "fix" him. I thought if I found the right therapist or doctor, supplement, medication or treatment, or…whatever…if only I could find the right help, Journey would be okay. The thing was, my son was an adult and he wasn't really asking for my help.

Chapter 13

*My sister is my better half, though now she has
a better half, who is better than I.*

~ Journey, Summer, 2010

Juxtaposition isn't meant to be a way of life, but my
life that summer was just that. Breaha had met a wonderful man, Zachary, and their wedding was to take
place just four weeks after Dawn's death. Likewise,
Josh had met a lovely woman and their wedding was
planned for later that summer in August. There was
the joy of preparing for two weddings and in stark
contrast, the sorrow of my sister's death and the fear
that gripped my heart when I considered Journey's
wellbeing. My feelings of fear and joy converged and
intersected. Optimism and pessimism collided on a
regular basis. I marveled how, in six short months,

my life had gone from happy and seamless to tense and unsettling.

Attending my client's births was a welcomed change of pace. Often, I would be called to a birth somewhere between midnight and 3 AM and could easily be gone for the next 24 hours. While it was exhausting in that respect, it was also fulfilling. Over the years I have trained my mind to be as single-focused as possible while at births. I was there to be of service in whatever way I could, and that required me to be present for my mamas, to hold the space of love for them during a potentially fearful and exhausting time. Being in the moment, holding love active and present, left little room for worrying about what was happening at home with Journey. So, while I was physically weary after a birth, mentally I was more at ease. And spiritually? Well, little compares to the awe one feels witnessing a baby take its first breath.

~

Rex and I felt vast relief when we found a therapist who felt certain, with time, he could help Journey. He acknowledged our deep concerns, discussed the option of medication vs. therapy or the use of both. His soft-spoken reassurance was soothing to my frayed nerves. He encouraged us to focus on getting through the first wedding and then he and Journey would start seeing each other twice per week.

As Breaha and Zach's wedding drew closer my anxiety escalated. A wedding ceremony is important, and I feared Journey would unwittingly do or say something to cause an upheaval. I knew with certainty that Journey would want to honor his sister and her husband at their wedding; it's just that there were times those days when his capacity for reason was questionable at best. His mental health seemed to have spiraled quickly downward in the month he had been home. Or maybe, living under the same roof, provided us with a more accurate depiction of his current state.

Breaha's wedding day came and by the grace of God the only major event of the day was that we added a son to our family.

A handful of our closest friends were aware of Journey's "condition" and spent extra time with him that night. Kathryn is a family friend and a member of the fellowship that studied with Dennis. She had known Journey since he was a small boy. I have always admired Kathryn's balance between intellectual knowledge and intuitive knowledge. I saw her with Journey a few times during the reception and felt grateful. A week or so after the wedding she called.

"Honey, Journey's been on my mind a lot since the wedding. How's he doing?" "About the same, I guess. Honestly Kathryn, I am at a complete loss as to how to help him. He has agreed to begin therapy, so hopefully that will help." Expressing empathy, she went on, "I don't know either, but just sitting next to him set my head spinning. We only shared a few snippets of conversation, and I know this is a weird analogy, but he reminded me of a monk on crack. It was like he was having all of these cosmic experiences but, rather than being linear, they were all layered on top of one another."

Thankfully, I was ignorant to Kathryn's thoughts during the wedding. Once the ceremony was finalized and the reception underway, Rex and I set our worries aside for the rest of the evening. It had been a long time since we had laughed and danced with such abandon.

After the wedding, Journey began therapy and slowly we began to see a difference. Not the same carefree, easy-go-lucky Journey, but not the secretive, meal skipping, eye rolling Journey either. I dared to hope that perhaps recovering his mental stability would be as simple as a safe, loving home and some good talk therapy.

Josh's wedding was another bittersweet day. It was a lovely outdoor wedding; the ceremony was beautiful and the party fabulous. It was heartwarming to see Josh so happy. Just beneath the surface however, like a low-grade fever, was my constant concern for Journey's wellbeing. He kept to himself that day. He was present for the ceremony (looking too thin and pitiful) but right after the ceremony he made himself scarce. At one point, I went off on one of the well-worn paths through the woods. I didn't want anyone to see me crying, and I was hoping to quiet my own heart by spotting Journey. I needed to know that he was okay.

Eventually I rounded a bend. It was dusk, but I saw him there, in a wooded glen. He was crying. Next to him was a plate of untouched food. His back was to me and I was certain he hadn't seen me or heard me coming. I offered a silent prayer; a plea for some peace, some healing for my son.

Silently, I backed away knowing that I was not welcome there. Back around the bend and well of out sight, I wiped my own tears and reminded myself to breathe. As I turned to make my way back to the party I heard Journey's soft voice calling after me, "I am okay, Mom. I am going to be okay." I cleared my throat and with a cheerfulness that I didn't feel, said, "I know, Journ. You're going to be okay." I stood there, trying to think of what to say or do next. I knew from many past experiences that forcing my will, however gentle, however well meaning, overt or disguised, didn't work. I didn't want to push, but I didn't want to leave him there alone, either. I heard from around the bend, "Bye, Mom. Go back to the party and enjoy yourself, okay?"

Chapter 14

Shortly after Josh's wedding, Journey told us that he was going back to Ann Arbor for the fall semester to take that final statistics class. My heart sank. I knew that it was a terrible idea. We reasoned, we cajoled, offered many other alternatives, even begged. "Stay here and continue your work with your therapist. Take it easy, play your guitar, maybe consider taking that class online or at MSU. But he had made up his mind and that was that. "I am going back to get my degree. It would be a lot less stressful if I could count on you to help me. Please quit trying to manipulate me into doing something else." I knew we were standing at a fork in the road. I wanted with all my heart to convince him to take my road. He didn't. He rarely did.

One morning, standing in the kitchen I tried one more time. "Journey, don't go back to Ann Arbor next week. Please. It's not good timing." I stood there with tears filling my eyes. He walked over and wrapped his arms around me. It was such a welcomed surprise. He held the embrace for a long time and then said quietly. "Mom, I know. This is scary...for me too. Please understand that I have to go."

Walking away from that moment, a faded memory came clearly into focus. It was a memory of holding Breaha as a newborn infant. The fierce love that I felt for her surprised me. I would have done anything for her and she was only three days old. Somehow, I knew as a mother that my life's lesson was to learn how to love my children purely; love them completely and yet have no attachment to the outcome of their lives. This idea of loving without attachment flies directly in the face of new-mother-hormones. Right after birth and for months following, a new mom is flooded with hormones that drive, insist really, that she love and protect her young at all costs. Maternal love could be named many things but "unattached" would never be one of them. And yet, here I stood decades later being asked again to let go.

~

Journey asked me to help him with the apartment search, assuring me that he would do the rest. It was late in the game to find optimum housing, but after days of looking online and talking to landlords, I found an apartment that Journey would share with two other young men. It would be affordable, he would be near campus, have his own room, and still be with other people. He agreed it sounded like a good plan.

That fall still stands out in my mind as insufferable. Journey decided since he was paying for a full semester, he might as well take a full credit load. "I can't imagine ever using a degree in economics. Our economy is so dismal, and it is only going to get worse." He agreed to take the statistics class to complete his degree, but his current fascination was biology and he intended to take four science classes in addition to the statistics class. Again, another bad idea. And again, he wasn't asking for our opinion.

One day while at work, Journey called and asked me to help him determine where a building was on campus. He had spent four years navigating that campus, and yet he was so disoriented, he didn't know where he should be? I began typing with shaking hands on my office computer, searching U of M's vast website. I knew that something was very wrong, and I made a mental note to search for mental health resources in Ann Arbor as soon as we got off the phone. Finally, I found and shared enough information that something clicked, and he said he knew where it was. He remembered I was still on the line and in a very upbeat and normal sounding voice said, "Okay, got it. Thanks Mom!"

I looked out of the large window from my office at the birth center, tears stinging my eyes. In the reception area behind me, one of the midwives was chatting happily with a new mom, gushing over her newborn. They were laughing and talking casually about a knitting pattern. Emotionally, I felt like I was being torn apart. I worked at a birth center; a place where new life began, and joy filled the very air. There I was, trembling with fear for my son and his future. It was agonizing. I wondered if I would ever feel light hearted again.

Chapter 15

A week into school, Journey insisted that he could not live where he was. The apartment had a terrible smell; something toxic in the heating system, or the walls. He couldn't bear to be there. After spending two nights sleeping on the steps of some church, he'd found another room to rent. He asked if I would come down and help him move his stuff. I suggested again that he come home. He could still get his deposit back and a refund for the semester. He could register for the spring semester. He hung up on me.

The next morning, I received a text asking me again to please help. My anger flared. I had a brief recollection of a teacher once telling me the difference between helping and enabling. What if I simply said no? If I refused to help him move, what would happen? I imagined him sleeping on the church steps and eventually getting picked up by the police. That might be a good thing. They would certainly take him to the hospital. My mind raced with all the potential "what-ifs" and in the end, I acquiesced. I couldn't say no.

I arrived at the appointed time the following morning, but Journey wasn't there. His stuff was in a neat pile with a note asking me to take it to the enclosed address. I tried calling, texting and calling again. No answer. I was furious and scared. It was getting late, so I decided to simply move the stuff and get back to Lansing. Journey's roommates of one week were careful about what they said but confessed that they didn't smell any toxic smells. As I closed the door behind me I wondered if Journey perceived body odor to be toxic, because there was a fair amount of that going on.

I took his few belongings (which seemed like a lot moving it myself) to the new address. It was on a dark street rather far from campus. His new roomies seemed like nice guys, and I stayed and chatted with them for as long as I could without seeming like a weirdo. I was hoping that Journey would show up before I left. He didn't.

I don't remember the drive home at all, but it was dark when I arrived, and Rex was out. I looked down at my hands and noticed they were shaking. I thought I was cold, so I decided to go out and soak in the hot tub. After ten minutes of being submerged in 104-degree water, my hands still shook. I had a moment of realization that nervousness was a real condition. Up until then, I thought when someone said they shook with fear it was figurative.

I surrendered to the shaking. I pleaded with the nighttime sky for answers. "God, please help Journey. Heal his mind. Let me do the mental illness. He has his whole life ahead of him. He's young and smart and caring. Please, God? Please heal him." I told God that I would give up an arm. Not enough? A leg then? My life! "Take me, God, and heal Journey. Please."

God was silent, and my breath continued to move in and out of my lungs. I was still alive but never felt more hollow or forsaken.

A prayer that I had prayed thousands of times since becoming a mother, came to mind. "Dear God, thank you for the privilege of being Breaha and Journey's mom. Guide me as I guide them. May your love and light protect them. Place their feet upon the path that you have chosen for them. Amen." The words tasted bitter on my lips. Really? This was the path the Creator had chosen for Journey? I felt a deep sense of betrayal rise within me.

That night I broke up with God. I'd had enough of the pretense of a divine intelligence that clearly was *not* intelligent and was heartless to boot. I stood there dripping wet and railed, "Screw you, God! I am through loving you." Sobbing and spent, I fell into bed, praying the rosary.

The following morning, I received a cryptic

message of appreciation from Journey. "Try not to worry. I bought a large, black trench coat to keep warm and to scare off anyone that thinks about messing with me." Never mind he weighed 125 pounds underneath it. After that text, days and then weeks passed without communication. Miraculously I was still his "friend" on Facebook, so I knew he was alive. Every day, sometimes several times a day, like an addict, I would get on the computer hoping to see evidence of his existence.

Chapter 16

October was upon us and so was Rex's and my 25th wedding anniversary. We had taken a big trip for our 20th and had no desire to be too far from home this year. We were planning a long weekend in northern Michigan, just far enough from home to be away, but close enough to get back if we needed to.

Early in the morning on the day we were going to leave, I decided to get in an early workout at the gym. Enjoying that virtuous post-workout feeling, I stepped into the shower. Just as I lathered up, my phone began to ring. I let it go to voicemail. As soon as the ringing stopped it began ringing again. My heart lurched. I stepped out of the shower onto the cold tile of the lady's locker room and fumbled for my phone. I didn't recognize the caller, but the area code indicated Ann Arbor. I mumbled some obscenity and sat down.

"Hello, Mrs. Montague-Bauer?" My mind vaguely (dutifully) noted that this voice was too chipper to be calling from a morgue or the police station. "Hi, I am calling from the University of Michigan Hospital. We have your son here. In the psychiatric unit." Her false cheerfulness, that was probably intended to offer reassurance, wavered. My ears began ringing. The sound and subsequent sensation was interfering with my ability to understand her. With the palms of my hands I cuffed at my ears a few times. I forced myself to suck in deep lungs full of air. "He didn't want me to call you, but I told him that I was going to anyway, and he could sue me later if he wanted to," her voice trailed off and ended with an uncertain chuckle.

Tears filled my eyes. I felt a surge of relief and hope. Journey was in the hospital. He was safe. "Perhaps he will get the help he needs," I thought. Directly opposing that relief was irrefutable dread. Once a person is in the mental health system they will receive a diagnosis, and that diagnosis would likely stay with them forever. I also knew that he would be medicated, and although that might affect his symptoms, it may drive whatever was causing his divided thinking even deeper. It felt like the truth to me when I heard a mental health professional suggesting that "psychosis can be an expression of 'deep, inner unhealed wounds,' and that psychiatric medications can numb the psyche and prevent those underlying issues from being dealt with." I had no idea what

Journey's deep, inner unhealed wounds could be, but I was willing to support whatever method would help him uncover it and experience healing.

I learned from the brief conversation with the social worker that Journey had been hospitalized four days prior, had already been assigned legal counsel, had been allowed a "trial" that took place over a hospital monitor screen, and that the judge had ruled in favor of the doctor's recommendation. Journey was now being medicated, against his wishes, and would be in the hospital at least two weeks for observation.

Four days after my arrival, there was a hearing regarding my stay. It was just a formality of course, because I was accused of being unstable by a team of respected doctors. I was well enough to read the pamphlet they gave me on Michigan regulations, and quote the portion that stated that a nonviolent person can refuse medication prior to their trial. I refused the medication, but a team of uniformed officers held me down while a nurse stuck a needle in my ass. This all occurred in a tiny windowless room.

You know, one of my greatest qualities is forgiveness. However, it is a certain type of holy to be able to forgive people for what they do to you while they are doing it.

~ Journey, Spring, 2010

We were asked to join the psychiatric team from Unit 9C at University of Michigan Hospital on Monday morning. She was sure the doctors would answer all of our questions then. "Okay, bye now! See you then!" she enthused. Either this woman didn't have children, and therefore could not know the impact of her call, or she could imagine all too well receiving such news and hid her own fear behind a cheerful disguise. In any case, I was left with a hundred questions and a mind too numb to formulate a coherent thought.

~

Our meeting was conducted in a bland looking conference room; white walls, no windows, an oversized table and enough chairs to seat an entire baseball team. Rex, Josh and I sat on one side of the table, while the "team" sat on the other. This team consisted of the head psychiatrist, two resident physicians, several medical students and the social worker that I had spoken with on Friday that had been assigned to Journey's case.

Journey knocked softly on the closed door and asked if he could be a part of the meeting but was told "not this time." My heart seized when I saw him there looking so vulnerable. My anger surfaced and subsided like a geyser; Journey was told "not this time" as we sat and discussed his life and future. While I understood the team's decision not to include him because we were going to talk about him, it still felt disrespectful.

The head psychiatrist began the meeting with questions like, "What kind of 'kid' was Journey?", "Did he present unusual as a child?" and "Did he make friends easily?" Patiently, like he was talking to non-English speakers, he told us they were trying to get whatever information they could to determine the best way to help Journey.

Eager to help, Rex and I offered that Journey was sensitive, funny, smart, well-liked, sometimes stubborn, often lazy, and yes, there were some things that were a bit different. "Like what?" the psychiatrist wanted to know. The students looked across the table expectantly, pens poised.

"Well, he has unusually acute hearing," I ventured. "When he was young he could 'hear' what was going on in the house even while he was asleep. I often wondered if some part of his awareness was able to stay conscious and alert even though he slept." The pens all remained suspended above their notebooks. The doctors looked up at me with well-practiced, neutral faces. One of the residents broke the awkward silence, "I would agree that Journey does possess hyper acute auditory perception." With only the tiniest bit of hesitation she went on saying that just the night before, she and a nurse were talking quietly at the nurse's station. Journey spoke up calling her by name, from his room down the hall. Politely and pointedly he let them know that he could hear and understand their conversation. There was another long, silent pause. I felt a modicum of gratitude and offered her a weak smile; at least I wasn't the only one receiving blank stares.

The mention of "Journey politely calling out from his room down the hall" triggered a strong wave of emotion. I wiped impatiently at my tears. A student, whose neutrality slipped for a moment to reveal compassion or perhaps pity, slid a box of tissues my way. Our eyes met briefly before he quickly looked away.

After some throat clearing, the doctor suggested we move on. "Anything else? Any other unusual behavior?" My mind went to three-year-old Journey and his visit from Jesus. I decided to skip that one. Then I recalled a time that I was playfully chasing Journey, and he fell. We were attending one of Dennis' workshops that was being held in a hotel conference room. Journey became restless and I took him out of the workshop to burn off a little energy before lunch and naptime. In the wide, heavily carpeted corridors between the conference rooms I stomped dramatically after a wound-up toddler. With my voice just above a whisper, I called after him, "I am going to get you!" while Journey ran away, squealing with delight.

In his excitement to outrun the boogie mama, he rounded the corner, lost his footing and began to fall. Then something remarkable happened. Time slowed down to a crawl. As Journey was toppling headfirst toward the solid corner, I watched frame by frame, as his head *passed through* the wall. I am not a physicist, but I observed in slow motion particles of matter, the molecules of my baby's head and the molecules of that steel-enforced corner, separate and completely avoid contact with each other. The only collision was Journey's chubby body tumbling two feet to the carpeted floor.

Time resumed its familiar tempo. I fell to my knees and gathered Journey close, the sound of my own blood flow rushing in my ears. He looked surprised but otherwise unharmed. Awkwardly, he reached up with a chubby hand and patted a tear from my cheek. I smiled weakly and offered a whispered prayer of gratitude: to him for his clumsy attempt to comfort me, to God for whatever miracle had just taken place, to Journey's guardian angel for protecting him from my ignorance, and to the world of matter for not being solid after all.

> *They say observing an electron changes its path.*
> *Eh, I'm not a physicist. A word of caution, never*
> *mind.*
>
> ~*Journey, Fall 2010*

In the white room with the oversized table, the neutral faces cleared their throats again. I felt certain that if they knew what I was thinking they would lock me up too. I reached for a safer topic, a concern that I had shared earlier but seemed to be overlooked. I began again, "The attack that took place on campus a couple of years ago? Journey's symptoms seem to coincide with that. Is it possible he is experiencing Post Traumatic Stress Disorder? Could PTSD trigger psychosis?" My train of thought was interrupted by one of the doctors asking if that attack had been reported to the police. Vaguely, I wondered why that mattered.

Shaking his head slightly, the lead doctor said that Journey's current situation was not likely related to the attack. When we questioned further, we were told that mental illness is a chemical imbalance, like diabetes. And, although chemical in nature, it can be triggered by a traumatic incident. That didn't make sense to me and I wanted to question him further, but my head felt like it was stuffed with cotton and I was having trouble forming logical thought. This team of well-trained professionals and their facility were considered innovative and cutting edge. Even so, we left with far more questions than we arrived with.

Before leaving, we had a brief visit with Journey. Several times he said that he was sorry. We assured him there was nothing to apologize for and that we loved him and would be there for him no matter what. We would figure out what was going on. Everything would be okay. As he stood up to leave we asked him if there was anything we could do for him. With tears in his eyes, he answered, "Pray for me." This was from our son that one week prior had reported he didn't believe in God. The fruit doesn't fall far from the tree.

Chapter 17

It's sad that things turned out this way. When I was inventing I never thought that I could die. I was forward-looking, and I even dreamed of getting married. I had dreams of being great. When I was a child it seemed impossible for things to be any other way. But now, I realize that I have led an average life and affected an average number of people.

Three months ago, I was diagnosed with psychosis and possible schizophrenia. I was taken into the Ann Arbor Mental Health system against my will and was studied. I was, in fact, crazy. After two weeks, they released me. I was still crazy.

Today I am writing what I believe to be my last words. I don't believe I am absorbing fat or protein and I have gotten progressively weaker as would be expected. The reason I am having this problem is because of things I did to myself while I was crazy. Now that I am sane, I regret the actions that led me here. I wish I had instead done anything differently. I wish I had done a million things differently. Hindsight is so much better than nowsight.

It has been three months since I started feeling this way, but because of my mental health record and circumstances beyond my control I am only now being tested for fat absorption. The test takes six days and I fear I will be too weak by the time they find out what is wrong for it to make a difference. I don't even really believe that there is a cure for the problem I have. I will now try to explain how I hurt myself.

I discovered that by making a weird face I could let food drain right through me. I thought that if I took minerals and let them drain through this way that they would have a supernatural effect.

Every morning I would make this face and take nutritional supplements with a bunch of water. I became paranoid and delusional and eventually was taken into the mental health system.

One day in the Ann Arbor hospital, I was facing a wet bum problem. I couldn't figure out why my bum would stay wet after I took a

*shower. So, I found in the bin of personal sup-
plies, a container of baby powder. After caking
it on, my bum started to burn. I was feeling dry,
but I began feeling concerned as well. I looked
at the container and read the ingredients. Corn
starch, and toxicil. I began running around the
hospital like a chicken without a head. I asked
the technicians "What do you do if you put on
too much baby powder?" They suggested that I
wipe it off or maybe take a shower, but since I
was crazy, I interpreted that they were giving
me an option that would help me and an option
that would hurt me. I believed that a shower
would soak water through the powder, drawing
more toxicil into my bum. I believed that the
tech knew this and was testing my whiles.*

*After wiping off most of the powder, I began
to feel panic, believing that the toxicil would
soak through my bum and enter my brain. I
turned and saw a box of tea bags my sister had
mailed to me. I grabbed a tea bag and ran it
under hot water. I placed it between my but-
tocks and clenched it there as I walked around.
I still have those stained underwear.*

*Later that night I was lying on the floor
because I was afraid of the magnets in my
bed. I thought the bed was trying to cook my
brain. I mean, it was plugged into the wall. it
had all these magnets and lights and switches.*

it freaked me out. Anyway, when the night nurse walked by she said, "I see you have your night-bag in." I believed this to mean, partially because she was Asian, that clenching a tea bag was culturally appropriate. I don't know why she said what she did, but I know I didn't make it up. I remember being crazy and I remember how it made me think. I remember believing people meant different things than they said. But I never thought I heard a sound when there was no sound. I knew the difference between sound and no sound.

I assumed that the nurse meant that a night bag should be worn outside of the rectum while a day-bag would be worn inside of the rectum. I was refreshed and felt cleaner with my night-bag, so I decided to test the day-bag. I went into my bathroom and placed a tea bag entirely into my rectum. It was a ginger tea and it burned like hell. I went into my room and sat in my chair. I reclined and imagined that I was soaring through space. I imagined that a friend was visiting me and placing imaginary jungle plants in the hospital so that the nurse, who was a cat, would feel at home. My eyes were closed, and I knew this was a sort of dream; I knew that there were no plants and that my nurse was human, but it still seemed real on some level. I dreamed that the president spoke to me and told me that he would get me out of the hospital.

The following morning, my sister came to visit. I told her that I was placing tea bags into my rectum. She smiled and said, "You have to be careful what you put in there because it is a sensitive area." I believed that she had sent the tea bags wanting me to discover a cultural secret that she had also discovered.

After being discharged from the Ann Arbor hospital, I believed that people were hinting to me to put other stuff up my butt. I am kind of embarrassed because there are girls I still like who I know will read this eventually, and it is embarrassing but I am not going to leave out the details of this story.

I thought that minerals like copper were building up in my colon and that by putting a silver conductive chain necklace in my butt I would clean it out somehow. I also thought that by attaching that chain to a bracelet around my junk that I would "complete the circuit", so to speak.

I know for certain that many famous people used what is called a butt plug. I have also seen with my own eyes a friend who wears a necklace with a leather cord down there. I am not going to name names, but the idea is not so far-fetched is all I am driving at.

Anyway, the idea to use a tea bag was dangerous and harmful. The string crossing the barrier of the sphincter acted as a wick to dehydrate my colon. With a dehydrated colon, the mechanism that allowed the food to drain through broke. I was making the face one day and I felt something inside snap. I felt my motivation to live drain away. It was the next day that I went back to the hospital. Since then I have spent most of my time in the Lansing Psychiatric unit where they have treated me for depression. I kept telling them "I am depressed because I am dying." They didn't believe me.

In retrospect, it's all kind of funny to talk about. Now, I'm conversely so grounded in reality that I am instead only aware of my physical body and not my mind. I wish I could again be so lost in my mind that I were unaware of my body. I wish I thought spirits were telling me I'd be fine after I died. I wish the TV were keeping better company. Everything is plain and superficial. My crazy adventure has ended, and what remains is as hollow as watching someone play a video game. Take me back into wonderland.

~Journey, Spring, 2010

Chapter 18

Two weeks later, Journey was discharged and came home. His face had filled out a bit and there was more color in his cheeks. Food tends to do that. Journey had always valued his independence and we did our best to support his autonomy while still making sure he was following the doctor's instructions.

A week or so after he was home, Journey started acting all snappy and tappy. I danced around the subject and then finally just asked him if he was still taking his medicine. He faltered and then finally said that he hadn't taken it that day. Aware that he had spoken the truth without telling me whether he had taken it yesterday or the day before, I invited him to sit down and talk. He declined my invitation. I repeated the party lines that we had heard; mental illness is like diabetes, you must take your medication to regulate your...brain chemicals? He sensed the interstice in my reasoning and shut me down.

Truthfully, I *was* having a hard time with the diabetes analogy. The first time I heard it, I listened and tried to make the connection. By the third, fourth or fifth time I had heard it from different doctors it began to sound more like a party line. Something doctors were taught to say, an answer to something that didn't have a clear answer.

I went on to caution Journey of the dangers of coming off his medication cold turkey. He cut me off. He was insistent that I help him right a wrong. He thought that perhaps psychosis was his karma for any harm he'd done in his life so far. I told him I didn't think it worked that way, but he became even more agitated and insisted that he needed me to listen.

I have always told myself that I am a good person, and guess I believed that I was. I did my best to follow a moral code. I tried to give my friends safe excitement. I was a good bad boy. I took them into construction sites, did non-addictive drugs with them, and played them my guitar. Sure, they could have been saving kittens, but let's be honest, we were all searching for a way to safely break the rules.

~ Journey, Summer, 2010

Journey confessed that in his senior year of high school someone had apparently dissed one of his friends. He and a few others decided that they were going to bring about retribution. They sneaked into the "offender's" family yard and put dye into their swimming pool. Tearful and frantic, Journey told me that he had to make amends. He insisted that it was his responsibility to pay back all the money that this prank had cost this family. He felt obligated to apologize to the classmate and her parents. Brandishing his checkbook, he told me that if I didn't drive him there he would take a cab. Obstinate and headstrong, I knew that he would do that or walk. I didn't want him out in the world alone, so I got my keys and we headed out in the cold November air so that Journey could make amends.

Despite our cautions against it, Journey stopped taking the medication. This, of course, was a bad idea because whatever symptoms a person was experiencing before are exacerbated by coming off medication abruptly. I have never been on psychotropic medications, but I have been told that coming off them suddenly can create a sense of agitation, fear and extreme anxiety.

This process has stripped me of much of my dignity. My initial reaction was to want to destroy things. I wanted to prove to myself that I still existed in this world, that I was not becoming invisible.

~*Journey, Summer 2010*

Absentmindedly, I fiddled with my keys. Pawing around in my purse, I realized I was stalling. Coming home had always felt like being embraced in a warm hug, but today my home seemed repellent, unapproachable even. Briefly, I considered pulling out of the driveway, making up an excuse that I had forgotten something at work.

A moment passed and then another. Finally, admonishing myself for being silly, I got out of the car and made my way up the walk. The house was quiet. I took a breath and opened the door. The men in my life were a tangled heap on the living room floor. Obviously straining, Rex had Journey pinned down beneath him. Red-faced, they both glanced up but neither spoke. In some other reality they could have been playing. Rex was a state champion wrestler in his youth and would often horse around with the kids, teaching them moves. But, this was no game and they were not horsing around. After an awkward moment, Rex slowly and deliberately said, "I am going to let you up and you are going to walk away." Journey begrudgingly nodded a barely-visible consent. Nimbly, they both rose to their feet and walked to opposite sides of the house.

Journey was the first to speak to me, asking me

to come into his room for a moment. Heaving an audible sigh, I opened the door to his bedroom. Before I could ask, he simply stated, "Dad has a lot of anger and I don't trust him." He gave a nonchalant shrug like what just happened was no big deal, "I was testing him." He motioned for the door, which was apparently an indication that my audience with his highness was over. Anger flared within me. It fueled a toxic mixture of hostility, fear and exhaustion. Apparently, it was too much to ask for just one boring, uneventful day.

Rex and I process the difficult things in life the exact opposite from one another. Usually, I withdraw and process inwardly until I have some clarity. Rex finds clarity by talking things out. I knew that he would seek me out when he was ready to talk. When he finally found me, I was surprised to see tears in his eyes.

"What in the world happened?" I ventured. Rex swallowed hard. His Adam's apple visibly working. "What the hell…?" he began. It was a rhetorical question, I knew he was still sorting it out in his own mind. Eventually he said, "I was sitting in the recliner, working on my computer. Journey got up from the couch and came toward me. He surprised me by saying, 'I think I am going to slug you in the face'."

Listening to this, my own face must have shown my surprise, because Rex went on, "I know. It was so weird and completely out of context. At first, I thought he was bullshiting, so I smiled, 'Yeah right,

Journ'. But he took another step toward me. His jaw was clenched, and his fists were raised, and I didn't know what to expect. I put my laptop down and I tried again, 'Journey, what is this about? We can talk like adults.' He kept coming toward me, so I stood up. I searched his eyes looking for some meaning, anything, but he just kept repeating that he wanted to hit me in the face. I told him he wasn't going to hit me because we had agreed as men to work out any issues we may have calmly, like adults. He smirked and said, "Yeah, but I want to slug you anyway." He never struck me, but he got within inches of my face and kept thrusting his fists. Eventually, I wrestled him to the ground. It was awful, honey." Feeling a bit of distance for once, I nodded compassionately and reached for Rex. Our roles temporarily reversed, I sat calmly and held my husband while he cried.

A few days later, while visiting Josh, Journey's anxiety escalated. He called 911, requesting an ambulance to take him to the hospital. Once there, he told the ER doctor that something was wrong with his colon and that he feared he was dying. Certain that it was malfunctioning and that he could no longer digest fats or proteins, he begged for help. He gave some specific details about the part of his damaged colon and its apparent deterioration. We had no idea where this was heading, but we could see that it wasn't going to be as straightforward as we had naively hoped.

Chapter 19

Journey was admitted to the Lansing psychiatric hospital, just two weeks after being discharged from Ann Arbor. This time, since he had been non-compliant with taking his daily pills, he was given an injection of an antipsychotic medication that is designed to last 30 days in the bloodstream and is intended to be given every four weeks. While he was there, I pleaded with the doctors to order other blood work and an endoscopy. They agreed to look for vitamin and mineral deficiencies and check for heavy metal toxicity, but they refused the endoscopy.

Journey insisted he was dying. He talked convincingly, begging us to help him. He was more afraid than ever and was eating next to nothing for fear he would make the "condition" worse. To appease his fear and to hopefully support him eating again, Rex and I promised we would take him for an endoscopy as soon as he was discharged. A physician friend of ours ordered the procedure and we took him directly from the hospital. The results were normal. Shortly after that, he received a diagnosis of somatic symptom disorder, a mental illness characterized by an otherwise healthy person obsessing over symptoms that have no medical basis.

> *There are two types of torture: psychological torture, and physical torture. I always thought physical torture would be worse, but lately I am not sure. Pain blurs the senses and dulls reality. Pain causes delusion. A broken spirit can occur with a sound mind.*
>
> *Ironically, most people diagnose me with "mistaken" broken spirit. In that case, a person only believes that things are hopeless. That would be a great inconvenience to his friends and family. If a friend of mine was falsely dispirited, I would respect him less. That is why I am offended and insulted that people claim that my suffering is an illusion. I am mourning the loss of myself. I am mourning my unborn children and unfulfilled destiny. My sadness is warranted because my loss is real.*
>
> ~*Journey, Summer, 2010*

Journey didn't want to come home to our house after leaving the hospital. Prior to his discharge, he asked for and received an invitation to stay at a family friend's home in Williamston. Their home is spacious, and we knew that Journey would be surrounded by loving friends, healthy food and acres and acres of nature.

The first night after being discharged, Journey called around midnight. He told us it felt like his skin was crawling and that his heart was racing. His legs felt numb and tingly and were twitching uncontrollably. His vision was blurry. He said, "I can't live like this. I just want to die."

Rex and Journey spoke several times that night. The following morning, we called the psychiatrist and learned that these symptoms were likely side effects of the injected medication. Journey was given a dose on the higher end of normal and there was nothing to do except wait for it to wear off. Rex called Journey at our friends' home and did his best to ease his mind, "Journ, listen. I spoke with the doctor. The symptoms you're having are likely related to the medication. Each day as the medication wears off you will begin to feel more like yourself." Journey wasn't convinced. He begged pitifully for Rex to help him. We drove out to Williamston to see if we could soothe him. It was painful beyond belief to witness his trembling hands, a body that couldn't be still, and a mind that was convincing him he was dying and would be better off if he did.

Journey insisted that Rex take him back to the

hospital. I recall watching as they drove down the long driveway back to the hospital, thinking this whole thing was a huge mistake. I feared the system that was designed to help him was making him worse. I collapsed to the ground and sobbed.

~

Three seems to be a significant number when it comes to psychiatric hospitalizations. One hospitalization could be a fluke. Twice, well there is still some leniency. Three times, and suddenly we began hearing phrases like "chronic and persistent mental illness" and "severe brain disorder with no known cure." So, while his medication was slowly wearing off, Journey was receiving counselling and simultaneously, being educated about his lifetime illness. One doctor even told Rex and me that it may take a few hospitalizations to 'break his will.' My face must have shown my dismay, because he quickly amended his comment to say, "What I mean to say is, we need him to come around to our way of thinking." I was silent. Waiting. He went on, "Our goal for him is to eventually learn that he has to stay on the medication. He needs to understand that he has a lifetime illness." We sensed what was coming next and, in stereo, we both said, "like diabetes."

Chapter 20

Our society has sadly lost trust for the individual,
and instead placed it in the institution.
~Journey, Summer 2010

During that third stay, Journey was told that he needed to apply for Medicaid. He still had hope for going back to school, getting his master's degree and paying for these trips to the hospital but someone told him it was possible, but unlikely. The phone rang late one night. Journey sounded weary, but there was a sense of urgency in his voice. "Mom, be truthful, do you believe that I have a future to look forward to?" "Journ, yes of course. You will recover. You will get to the other side of this, I am certain of it."

Motivated by Journey's desperate hope and my own conviction, I spent hours upon hours looking for alternatives to treating mental illness. What little information that was available was difficult to find, and if there were clinical trials, they often weren't performed in the United States and therefore not approved by the FDA. Then, to make things more challenging, I was met with resistance whenever I brought up any of these ideas to the doctors treating Journey. It was like they all had drawn a imaginary but very deep line. Allopathic medicine and naturopathic medicine, it seemed, didn't play well together. This didn't make sense to me then and it still doesn't make sense. When a person is struggling physically or mentally, shouldn't they be given all opportunities to get better? Shouldn't these two ends of the spectrum of care still work together to serve patients? For example, one day, I came across a research paper stating the value of adding fish oil supplements to the diet of people taking antipsychotic medication because it helped to mitigate the unwanted side effects of the medication. Since unpleasant side effects are a large complaint of folks taking these medicines, it seemed this would be an example where both traditional and nontraditional modalities would work hand in hand, without compromising the effects of either treatment.

One of my friends asked me if I was against medication. The truth for me was and is, "I value medication, but not as a first action." I wanted Journey's doctors to ask questions. I wanted them to leave no stone unturned before they proclaimed to us that Journey had a lifetime illness that came with a devastating prognosis.

Chapter 21

Christmas of 2009 was the first holiday spent without Journey. We went up to the adult psych unit to visit him. Waiting in the bleak area outside the elevators, our moods were subdued. There was an artificial Christmas tree with paper ornaments and no lights. It was still a new concept to me that a string of Christmas tree lights could be used as a weapon to harm oneself or others.

Journey sat across from us, not wanting to meet our eyes. His hair hung unwashed, a worn hoodie and a pair of cotton hospital scrub pants draped in wrinkles off his rail-thin body. We tried for small talk and failed. Eventually we simply told him that Christmas was about family and being together. We would wait for him to get home and celebrate Christmas then. He thanked us and stood up looking relieved; probably to give up the pretense of visiting.

On the way home I couldn't help but wonder, "If I am feeling this desperate, what must Journey be feeling? What is happening to our son?" I kept asking but there were no answers.

That New Year's Eve we spent time with family friends and their children. We played games and did our best to keep our hearts and minds on appreciation. We left shortly after midnight but instead of driving home, we found ourselves at the hospital, parked outside the Behavioral Health building. I was behind the wheel and don't recall making a conscious decision to drive there, but in that moment, it felt like the only place to be. Over the years, Rex and I'd formed our own traditions around New Year's Eve and they had little to do with partying or watching the ball drop in Times Square. Typically, we would spend the evening together or with a handful of friends. Good company, good food and libations were all important of course, but the primary focus was on reflection and appreciation.

As midnight approached we would light a candle, turn off our devices and spend some time in quiet contemplation. We would give thanks for the blessings of the past year and set intentions for the coming year.

I found a place to park and cut the ignition. The lamplight in the parking lot cast a feeble glow on the darkened windows of the building. I imagined Journey sleeping soundly. That was one of the benefits of being snowed on medication. Rex reached up and wiped away my tears with the back of his hand. There was nothing to say, so we simply held hands in silence. Eventually, Rex offered a heartfelt prayer for Journey's healing. We thanked God for creating the space for a full recovery. We prayed to be guided in that healing process and to learn whatever it was we needed to learn from this experience. We prayed for all the residents, and for the staff that was taking care of them.

Without a word being spoken between us, we knew it was time to go. I started the car and silently we made our way home.

Chapter 22

*Some people proclaim with pride that they don't
need faith. Maybe they are stronger than me,
or maybe they haven't seen what I have seen.
Regardless of what is true, faith that "all is well"
is a blessing.*

~ Journey, Summer, 2010

When I was not pleading, or ranting or trying to bar-
gain with God, I would sometimes quiet myself and
listen. Listening used to be easier back when I liked
God. Back when I believed that God cared about me
and my family and actually gave a shit. But there
were still times when my eyes burned from spending
hours at the computer looking for solutions or from
crying. In those instances, I would sit myself down
and stay there until I found a small measure of peace.
In those moments, I would ask "What is my part?

What am I supposed to be learning?" I think I was hoping for some insight, something I had overlooked that would heal Journey. What I heard though, time and time again, was simply, "Be patient. Trust."

Since Journey didn't want visitors at that time, we communicated with letters or cards, or the occasional phone call. One evening I drove to the hospital to drop off a card for him. While in the reception area, waiting to be buzzed up the psych unit, I had an encounter with another young man who may have been a patient there. He appeared to be confused. He was talking to himself under his breath; short, ambiguous syllables. He looked up and we made eye contact. He smiled brightly and patted the seat next to him, beckoning for me to join him.

Six months ago, I would have been afraid of this man, although I wouldn't have admitted it. I probably would have averted my eyes and pretended not to notice his gesture. Now I simply felt compassion. I stood up and walked over and took the seat next to him. After a moment, he took my hand and held it tenderly. His hands were smooth and cool, his fingers long and slender. They were slightly tanned even though it was mid-January. He closed his eyes for the span of a breath and then opened them and looked directly at me. He had stunningly beautiful blue eyes. There was a deep calmness in him that I rarely see in the world around me. It was a direct contradiction to his apparent state just moments before. Holding eye contact, he said with perfect articulation, "What is happening to your son is not your fault. He will figure out what he needs to, just remember it's not your fault." He let go of my hand and went back to his own internal dialogue. I remained next to him even though he had clearly moved on from our interaction.

The elevator door opened, and the psych tech stepped out. He offered a tired smile as he took the envelope that I brought for Journey. Heading for the door, I heard him address the man in the waiting area. Stepping out into the bright winter day, it occurred to me that I had never told the man I had a son.

~

During that stay, the only person Journey wanted to see was Aunt Susan. Susan was a family friend and had known and loved Journey since he was an infant. As painful as it was to be excluded from comforting Journey myself, I was eternally grateful that Susan was there for him. Susan was a social worker and employed at Community Mental Health (CMH) at the time. She was more familiar with psychosis and I suspect it didn't frighten her to the core like it did me. Periodically, Susan would give me small details of their visits. "He asked me to bring him some milk, he seems to be eating a bit more today" or "He asked me to sing to him while I stroked his hair."

Sometime later, Rex asked Journey about his refusal to see me. "She is so worried all the time, Dad. And, I can't stand to see the sadness in her eyes." After that, I put more effort into being cheerful, or at best neutral, when I was around Journey. It didn't work very well. Regardless of whether my lips were turned up or not, Journey had an excellent pulse on what I was feeling. He'd always had a way of knowing my internal workings, sometimes better than I knew myself.

On January 15th, 2010 Journey was discharged from his third hospital stay. The doctor agreed that the last dose of psychiatric medication was too high and gave him an injection of 39 mg instead of the 156 mg he received the month before. Journey was given the shot and all of us were instructed that he should go to CMH in one month for the next injection.

The doctor that performed the endoscopy today, had eyes that were pure blue; he was wise and intelligent. He was rather harshly objective though, and his mouth made the deepest frown I've ever seen. It was a frowny face like a cartoon, but not funny. He acted rude, confrontational, and insulting. He was cold to protect his feelings, because he couldn't bear to believe that bad things happened to good people. It made me sad to show him how weak I really was, and I wished he did not have to see any suffering. I have had a colonoscopy, a barium enema, and

a series of blood tests so far. They have found I
have a low serum plasma and low vitamin D.
The other tests were normal. It is for that reason
that I have little hope for salvation. I am cur-
rently eating 100 grams of fat per day so that
they can test for absorption. I don't know if a
procedure exists that can fix me, but I doubt it.
~ Journey, Summer, 2010

Before coming home, we took Journey for another
procedure; this time a barium swallow which is a
medical imaging procedure used to examine the
upper gastrointestinal tract. Neither Rex nor I
believed anything was wrong with his GI tract upper
or lower, but it seemed worth the cost of the procedure to give Journey reassurance that he wasn't dying.
It didn't work. He thought the doctors just couldn't
find his particular issue. Journey had always had a
sharp mind and clear intuition. I suspect this made
it harder to accept that he was wrong about this one
thing. On every conversation topic except this one, he
was cogent and persuasive.

Why did my body break? No doctor has told
me. I will probably never know what specifically
went wrong, and why. all I know is that I am
out of the race.
~ Journey, Summer 2010

With every return trip from the hospital, Journey seemed to spiral further into depression. Each time, he seemed more distant and I found it harder to reach him. He maintained there was no hope for him, insisting he was too broken and would never get well. He chastised me every time I offered encouragement. Frustrated with his constant yammering about his imminent death, I reminded him of something he had told me long ago. Journey was probably eight or nine years old when he found me in the garden and announced that he had experienced a vision of himself as an adult. A "vivid daydream" is what he called it. "I was in my twenties and looked handsome in a suit and tie. I had a briefcase like Dad's, and I knew that I had important work to do. I looked handsome and happy."

"Hmm, that sounds nice, Journ" I said absentmindedly. He stood there, his thin body blocking the late afternoon sun. He waited expectantly. Clearly, he had anticipated more of a response. I turned away from the weeds that were ravaging my garden. I sat back on my heels and gave him my full attention.

"Well, I just thought you'd want to know that," he shrugged his bony shoulders.

"Sure. That's good son," I smiled. "I'm certain that you will grow to be a happy and successful man someday."

"A businessman" he corrected. Our eyes locked briefly. His brown eyes a mirror of my own, looked at me intently, and then apparently satisfied, he ran back toward the house. It was a brief moment in time and I probably would have forgotten about it entirely if I hadn't written it in my journal.

When no amount of logic or medical testing appeased Journey's conviction that he was living his last days, I reminded him of the vision he'd had as an eight-year-old boy, seeing himself all grown up and happy. He looked at me with disdain. "Jesus, Mom. I made that up. I made it up so that you wouldn't be sad about me, about my future."

"But…why would I be sad about your future, Journey? You were a happy, healthy eight-year-old."

He looked at me like I was from another planet. "God, you still don't get it, do you?" He dismissed me with a wave of his hand, "Never mind. Just forget it."

Maybe very few people have imagined a future with me in it. Probably a number of them less than ten. I couldn't even picture myself in the future.

~Journey, Summer, 2010

Chapter 23

That first day Journey was home, he, Rex and I were all in the living room, trying to be together as a family. What for years was the most natural thing in the world had now become stilted and awkward. None of us were good at small talk, but no one knew how to broach the big talk either. Rex was reading, I was writing in my journal and Journey was sitting calmly. A few moments later I looked up and saw tears running down Journey's cheeks. Rex acknowledged his sadness and asked him how we could support him. Journey looked from me to Rex and back and surprised us both by saying "You both look *so old*." We busted out laughing. That certainly wasn't what I was expecting. The tension eased a fraction, Journey went on, "I am serious. You have both aged ten years. I'm so sorry. He choked on a sob, "I'm just really sorry." We told him again that there was nothing to apologize for. We agreed that it had been stressful for all of us. Smiling, I said, "Clearly we're on a fast track to learning something. God, it'd be helpful if we knew what it was."

In a two-month span, we asked for (and I am embarrassed to admit resorted to pleading for) every test known to modern medicine that looks at the GI tract from one opening to the other. All the tests came back normal.

Rex and I began to wonder if something more happened when Journey was attacked at school. We knew that he'd been knocked unconscious. He'd said only for a moment, but if he were unconscious how would he have known? He had been trying to "fix" himself with fasting and cleansing and weird posturing ever since. He was fixated on a damaged colon; the sigmoid, the part of the colon that meets the rectum. We wondered if perhaps he had been raped or sexually abused during that attack, but when we brought it up, Journey denied it.

Journey continued to insist he was fragile and weak and getting weaker every day. He attempted to rectify any perceived mistakes he had made in his short life, thinking that perhaps he was being punished by God. After writing a sizeable check to the swimming pool family, he didn't openly discuss this theory, but occasionally, he would make a call or email a friend to apologize for some perceived wrong he had done.

He wrote a daily blog, listened to music, watched TV and read vast articles online trying to diagnose his own "fatal" condition, believing his only hope was to find a remedy to save his own life. During that time, and for several months to follow, he didn't leave the house. Vehemently believing that his body could not process protein or fat, he refused to eat anything that contained either. To eat those things, Journey believed, would further burden his failing system. We told him the brain consist of primarily fat and needs high quality fat to function properly. But of course, this was using rational thought, and when it came to that subject, Journey was anything but rational.

Eventually, we found a therapist who specialized in Cognitive Behavioral Therapy. This doctor, bless his heart, agreed to come to our home for weekly sessions with Journey. Good naturedly, Mr. Friend (as Journey referred to him in his blog) would come over and sit in Journey's dank bedroom for their weekly sessions. Journey enjoyed his visits and thanked us for the investment, even though he thought it was a lot of money to pay for a friend.

Chapter 24

I keep staying up later and later. It's 5:00 AM.
When I dream, I dream that I am going blind.
Every night I see less and less in my dreams. All
my friends come to me and wave their arms in
front of my face and ask why I can't see them
anymore. I have no answer for them.
                          ~ Journey, Summer, 2010

Other than his high school friend Carlos, Mr. Friend,
and the very occasional visitor, Rex and I were the
only people Journey talked to with any regular-
ity. I would go to work and almost as soon as I got
home, would go into his room and visit. We would
talk, or he would read to me what he had written
on his blog, or something from his favorite website,
Reddit. We watched TV and basically just hung out
together. Sometimes we had real conversations; about

relationships, regrets and about life and death. He said that these conversations might help me after he was gone. Although believing he was living his last days, he still had his wit and tried to make our visits fun. One time we got on a laughing jag after he joked about putting his cremation ashes into some brownies and feeding them to the funeral guests. I laughed with him because it seemed like a little brightness would be helpful, but that night I shoved my head into my pillow and cried myself to sleep.

A couple of times I refused to have conversations about his impending death, citing the strength of the mind/body connection. If a person spent all their waking thoughts believing they were dying, couldn't that in fact contribute to it? Journey scoffed at my "logic" and told me he couldn't believe all the bullshit I believed and called faith.

After one particularly heated conversation, he dismissed me angrily. "I would rather be alone and lonely than listen to your new age ideas, which are total crap!" The tension was high, and we threw angry words back and forth until exasperated I stormed out of his room, slamming the door behind me.

Even though it was only 8 p.m. I crawled into bed. Fitfully, I tried for sleep and failed. About twenty minutes later, I heard the soft chords of Journey's guitar. He was standing outside my bedroom door singing softly. It was a beautiful, melodic piece that I suspect he was making up on the spot. His voice was low and soothing. He sang to me that I need not worry. "Everything" he hummed, "was going to be okay."

~

Before falling asleep that night, I asked God to send me a dream. My daily life was tumultuous and so unpredictable. I asked for something, anything, that would be true and that I would know was directly from Source. I had two dreams that night that I remembered long enough to write in my journal.

In the first dream I was an observer. I was not in the dream, I simply watched objectively as a very vivid life experience unfolded before me. I witnessed a soul decide on its life lessons before being born, and then grow up and live its purpose. This person's life was difficult. There were daily challenges and a lot of physical pain and sickness. The mother was sad and crying and prayed incessantly for a different outcome. I knew, as the objective observer, that everything was happening according to the soul's plan.

In the second dream I was not an observer but an active participant. Journey was a baby, maybe a year old. He toddled over and bit me on the arm. I gently told him we mustn't bite. Then I was nursing him. I looked at his sweet face and felt a huge rush of love for him. The sun was shining in his eyes, so with my free hand I shaded his face from the brightness of it.

As I gazed at his face, I was overcome with profound joy and love.

There was no need for interpretation with the first dream, its meaning was obvious. It was a reminder that despite the apparent reality, things are following an unseen plan.

The second dream reminded me that I was, and am, a good mother. I had done nothing wrong to cause Journey's pain and confusion. Despite some of the books I had read linking a mother's love (or lack of it) to mental illness, I knew with certainty, that I loved Journey then and now as purely as a mother could.

Chapter 25

An old friend visited today. It was like admitting I'd lost the greatest competition of my entire life. Despite that I enjoyed seeing him, it made me feel miserable. I loved hearing about his success, and I don't feel as if my accomplishments thus far are much less impressive than his, but to admit that I will be dropping out of the race killed me.

I am not finished. I have not written every word. And now it is being cut from me. Or I am being cut from it. I am invisible, and I shall fade like the smoke from a joint, getting people high for a while and then forgotten. I love my friends. It gives me honor to be respected by people of high status. It just reminded me that I'm as good as dead. My creativity is gone, and nobody wants to be reminded of how a person can turn into a husk.

~Journey, Summer, 2010

Days, weeks and then months passed. Journey was surprised every day that he woke up instead of dying in his sleep. Some evenings he was so sure that it was his last, he would ask me to sleep in the recliner in his room next to his bed so that he wouldn't have to die alone. That spring I spent as many nights in the recliner next to Journey while he slept as I did in my own bed.

One morning Journey was mocking me, "Oh, you are so enlightened, Mom," followed by eye rolling. "You can't be enlightened until you have faced death, until you have looked it square in the eye and remain at peace. You haven't done that yet." Apparently, he gave it some more thought, because later that evening he knocked softly on my office door, "I may have been wrong about what I said earlier. As hard as it is for me to know that I am dying, I am pretty sure watching your own child die is more painful. Sorry, Mom."

To keep our marriage from being consumed by stress, Rex and I would make time for monthly dates. One afternoon while Rex was out, he called spontaneously and asked if I wanted to meet him for dinner and then a movie. The idea of getting out of the house and not having to make a meal was delightful.

I stood in front of my dresser staring blankly

at my reflection. I hardly recognized myself or the life we were living. I picked up one pair of earrings, decided against them and fumbled for another. Eventually, I decided on no earrings, opting for some hastily applied lipstick instead. Nothing looked or felt right. Journey wandered in to keep me company while I paced around my room, trying to focus on getting myself out the door. His stomach was growling so voraciously I could hardly focus on anything else. I couldn't remember the last time my stomach growled with hunger. I felt a stab of guilt and a lot of sadness. I did my best to shelve those feelings for the time being and forced myself to smile. "Is there anything that sounds good? We are going for Indian food…. How about some "not rotten karma"'? He smiled at the joke, his name for Navratan Korma, and shook his head no.

Then he surprised me by asking what I was so furious about. I looked at him dumbfounded. "I am not angry," I said, tears pooling in my eyes. "I am sad."

"Maybe on the surface, but just underneath that, you are pissed off," he insisted. We went back and forth, Journey insisting that I would feel better if I dealt with my rage. He tried insulting me. He provoked me. "Come on Mom, just let it out. I can handle it, I promise." I looked for rage, but I couldn't find it. "Really, Journey, I'm just feeling sad right now, okay?" And then after a brief pause, I said, "Maybe you're projecting your feelings on me? Maybe you're the one who's angry?" With as much calmness as I could muster, I told him it was safe to reveal his anger. He could let it out and I would hold a safe space for *him*.

He looked me square in the eye, his head shaking ever so slightly, "Someday when you find your rage, remember this conversation." He sighed and walked away.

———

Chapter 26

Journey had been experiencing rocky terrain in most of his relationships and ours was no exception. Many times, he was rude or distant and sometimes acted downright mean. I knew that wasn't Journey's true nature. He was a kind and gentle person. I reminded myself that it was the illness that caused him to be sharp, edgy and hurtful. As I watched my son move in and out of madness I was forced to say goodbye repeatedly. One time I even thought that death would be easier than insanity. When someone dies, you say goodbye once. When someone is not in their sound mind, you are forced to say goodbye slowly, a hundred tiny heartbreaks. Remembering that thought still triggers guilt in me. I wonder if thinking that horrible thought and then having the audacity to voice it out loud, could have played a part in it happening?

My only visitor is my mom. Lately it seems as though she is having a difficult time.
                    ~Journey, Summer, 2010

One day in mid-June, I came home from a birth and stopped by Journey's room to check on him. He ignored my tap on his closed door. I assumed that he was sleeping or had his headset on and went about getting ready for bed.

Eventually he came out of his room, but when I addressed him, he looked away without a word. I was too tired to deal with games, so I simply bid him good night and went to bed. Days passed, and Journey continued to ignore me. I stomped my feet and demanded to know what I had done to offend him. I was furious and told him so. He acted like I wasn't there.

He would speak with Rex though. He was lucid, communicative, and even jolly at times. "Screw you," I thought. I called a friend and scheduled a walk in the park and a movie afterward.

The summer dragged on. Still not a word from Journey even though we lived under the same roof, and still he barely ate. I fantasized that maybe he was getting up and eating at night. For several nights I planted an invisible trap. I placed a single strand of hair between the side by side handles of the refrigerator to see if the doors had been opened. I wanted to know if he was going into the kitchen at night for a snack. He wasn't.

I became acutely aware of the pain that mothers face watching their children starve. I felt compassion for those mothers, prayed for them and their hungry children. I never in my wildest dreams could've imagined living in the world of plenty, and still watching day by day as my son became more and more emaciated.

As summer wore on toward fall Journey seemed to talk less about dying and sometimes even spoke of his future. Eventually he went out more. He even started going to his therapy appointments in Okemos. One day exactly 90 days after he stopped talking to me, he addressed me directly and in a friendly way. I responded similarly to this abrupt conversation as I had to his sudden decision to ignore me. Incredulous, I asked him what gave him the right to ignore me for three months and then act like nothing had happened? The answer he gave for his verbal absence started with a question "Mom, do you remember back in the spring when I encouraged you to go to your yoga class or visit with your friends? Go on more dates with Dad?" Yes, I did remember but wondered what it had to do with my question. I wanted an answer, dammit. Calmly he continued, "You needed a break. You were spending all of your time with me and it was wearing you out." I stood there with my mouth open, wanting to reproach him, say something. He walked over and placed his finger under my chin and gently closed my mouth.

"It worked, didn't it?" It had indeed worked. Not long after being dissed by Journey, I began to resume more of a social life. He smiled a sad smile. What had originally seemed like the act of a selfish ass had been a conscious gift.

Chapter 27

It feels so good to be in public. Sure, there are rude, mean people, but there are also kind people and curious people and knowing people and they all show me something about what is happening to me. Locked in my room I have no perspective.

~Journey, Summer, 2010

In Mid-September, Journey and Mr. Friend seemed to have a breakthrough. Journey, reported Mr. Friend, was clearer than he had ever seen him. One day shortly after that, Journey returned from one of his appointments and found that he was locked out of the house. "I am just leaving an appointment, Journ. It is going to be at least 90 minutes before I am home."

"Don't worry about it, Mom. It looks like the neighbors are home. I'll wait there."

As it was, our neighbors were hosting the bi-monthly Neighborhood Watch meeting. Lawn chairs were strewn across their lawn as neighbors milled around and eventually settled down. The focus of the meeting was the recent crimes in our neighborhood. There had been several break-ins and there was even a shooting that had resulted in a death.

That night, Journey complained of severe chest pain. In hindsight, it was probably anxiety, a panic attack. Before we could address it in the morning, Journey was gone. He had taken a cab to the hospital emergency room telling the ER doctors that he thought he was having a heart attack. He returned that afternoon with printed material on bipolar disorder and schizophrenia.

Journey and I were up most of that night. I figured he had a lot to discuss with me following three months of silence. There were moments of brilliant clarity and then he would lapse into confusion. At one point, in the wee hours of the morning, he was seized with panic. "Mom, I feel my mind slipping again. What should I do?"

"Let's start with something to eat. How about a grilled cheese?" I offered. He shook his head. "Severely restricted calories for a prolonged period, combined with no sleep would cause anyone's mind to slip, Journey. C'mon, I'm hungry. Let's go find something to eat." He contemplated my suggestion, but ultimately refused my many offers of food.

He confided that he could literally feel himself slip in and out of madness. While "there" many things made sense to him. There were things he *just knew*, but often that knowledge did not translate into this dimension. "There are several dimensions and each one has different rules of physics and even different languages. One of them," he said, "is a language of geometric shapes and symbols. Some of them are scary, because they are unfamiliar, but mostly they are exhilarating and make this world seem mundane and without meaning."

Sometime during that all-night conversation Journey heard me, really heard and understood that his colon was not broken, at least not physically. He looked so relieved and said that if that were true it was both thrilling and terrifying in the same moment. He could then see how all the people who had been telling him that he wasn't physically sick were right. They were speaking what they knew to be true and were really just trying to help him. He apologized for being a pain in the ass and we laughed.

I dared to hope that, perhaps just like that, he had seen the light and would now go on to live his life. He excused himself saying that he had to go write something down. Five minutes later, he returned and denied everything he had just acknowledged. He was gone again, back to a world that didn't translate to this one. In that moment, I understood the saying which is often spoken in a derogatory way, "That guy's not all there." A part of Journey was sitting on the couch across from me, and a part of him was clearly somewhere else, essentially not all here and not all there.

After a few hours of sleep for me, and none for Journey, I left to go out to Williamston for a sleepover with a few girlfriends. Two out-of-the-ordinary things happened that day.

The first was a voicemail from a woman named Cathy. I had no idea who this woman was, but her message indicated that she was trying to reach a friend of mine. I wasn't going to call a stranger and give her my friend's contact information, but I did call my friend. "Oh, my gosh," she enthused, "Cathy is the intuitive that I told you about!" And then, "Why did she call you? How did she get your phone number?" Neither of us had any idea. She explained that Cathy had helped her and so many others. I must have sounded skeptical because she went on patiently, "Cathy is a down-to-earth woman, much like you and me. She was raised in a Catholic family and realized as a young girl that she knew things that other people didn't. Fortunately for her, instead of telling her she was the devil's spawn, her priest encouraged her to develop her God given gift. She ended up helping many people in her church and has helped people ever since." Maybe she can shed some light on Journey's situation?" I asked her if she had mentioned me or Journey to Cathy. She assured me that she had not. I was doubtful but had already agreed to saw off my arm in exchange for healing, so a phone call to a stranger that "knew things" wasn't really that big of a stretch.

The second thing that happened on my way to Williamston wasn't that out of the ordinary, but the results were unmistakable.

As I was wondering how Cathy got my number and if she could indeed shed some light on Journey's illness, I pulled my car to the side of a deserted country road. The warm September sun felt glorious. For the umpteenth time, I prayed for Journey's well-being. "God, please help me help Journey..." The warm setting sun drew me out of my car. I walked over to the edge of a field and fell to my knees. I fingered the delicate leaves of a bean plant. Its edges were starting to brown, but still it was perfect. One seed had turned into a plant full of food. I am not a biblical scholar by any means, but I recalled a scripture about lilies in the field and how the Creator tends to every little detail of life; flowers, bean plants and people. I, a beloved child of God, should not worry about a single thing.

I was at the edge of a farmer's field, but I felt like I was at the edge of the world as I knew it. I could stay here on this precipice, distraught and terrified, or I could take a leap of faith. I looked down at myself, hands shaking, afraid. I chose to leap. To the setting sun, to the farmer's field, to God, I professed that I surrendered. I had done everything in my power to help my son but so far, I had failed.

"Here he is, God: our beloved son, Journey. I place him and all his affairs into your care. I don't know how to help him. I hope that you really do exist and that you love him as much as I do." In my mind's eye and in my heart, I placed Journey on the altar before God.

A few moments later I pulled into my friend's driveway and was soon embraced by three of my closest friends. Life had been more difficult than I could have imagined, and yet one thing was for certain; I had a prolific circle of friends and family that supported me. I knew that at any time night or day, there were dozens of people I could call if needed. Even in my distress, I recognized the great gift that was. One of my friends held me at arm's length, "Wow, you look different. Lighter somehow." She smiled and hugged me to her. I had to admit that I felt freer than I had in years.

The next morning when I got home, *Journey was gone*. We had no idea where he was. He left no note. The frightened young man who hadn't left the house in seven months and only recently ventured out once a week to therapy appointments had taken flight without a word.

I shook my fist. "What the hell, God? Is this your way of taking care of Journey? *Where is he*?" I choked on my own sobs. What a fool I had been to surrender my son to an invisible, fictional God that clearly didn't care about my son or me. I hauled my pillow and a blanket out to the living room. I couldn't bring myself to go to bed. I was holding vigil. It was one of the many times I had to let go, though I didn't know at the time, if I was letting go of my hope for Journey's recovery or Journey himself. Even though I had broken up with God again, I couldn't help myself from falling on my knees in supplication. Old habits die hard.

Chapter 28

I decided to call Cathy, the medical intuitive, much to Rex's indignant head shaking. Finally, he said, "If you are going to be vulnerable and listen to her perspective, at least let her do all of the talking. Don't give her anything to bait you with." We set an appointment for two days out. Three days after Journey's disappearance.

The morning of our phone appointment with Cathy, I wrote down a few questions as she had instructed. Where was Journey? What was his diagnosis? What did he need for recovery? Would he recover? How could we most support his healing? I prayed to a God that I doubted daily, asking to know if this woman was a quack. And if she wasn't, to guide her insights.

Cathy first asked for a name, an age and a location if known. We gave a name and an age, but we confessed that we did not know where Journey was. After a brief pause, she asked us if we thought that he was in a hospital. We didn't know. Her second statement got both of our attention. "Well something has happened to set his mental health on its ear." No shit.

After that statement, Rex sat up and came to attention. I had so many questions about how she knew what she knew, but I waited until closer to the end of the conversation to ask her about that. I stuck to our original questions. I am paraphrasing of course, but essentially, she observed a happy, well-adjusted college student and then quite abruptly she saw someone pretending to be okay who wasn't. She noted that Journey had always been a perfectionist. He put a lot of pressure on himself to do well and then something happened to "tip the scale." She asked us if we knew what that might have been. Despite our original decision to keep our lips zipped, I did offer that he had been attacked at school. Perhaps it was that? She was silent for a long moment and then concluded that the attack may have been the trigger. "There were several men that were up to no good that night. It is by the Grace of God that Journey is alive today." I reconsidered making up with God again. Wishy-washy me. Cathy told us that most of the trauma was below conscious awareness. She suspected that Journey was either on drugs at the time, knocked unconscious or both. "Some part of him died that night. His innocence. But something more. A part of him left and hasn't fully returned."

"Let's look at his current environment. We'll look as though we are seeing through his eyes." She maintained that it looked like a hospital setting. She admitted the next part didn't make sense to her at all. She was seeing random letters, "E, C, A, D… this doesn't make sense to me, but this appears to be what he is seeing." Rex rolled his eyes. Since Cathy was on speaker phone, I gave him the silent hairy eyeball, which translated to, "Just listen with an open mind or leave!"

She then proceeded to gently but firmly scold me, "Mitzi, you have got to get your fear under control. It's like this great pulsing energy that makes it hard to experience anything else." Rex's lips turned up slightly, but he was quiet. I sighed and admitted that I felt afraid for Journey most of the time. She went on, "It isn't helping. It is making it harder for him, in fact."

She conveyed that his doctors suspected bipolar or schizophrenia but that neither seemed accurate in her opinion. She may have sensed my mistrust of the current mental health system, because she continued by reminding us that the doctors and nurses had Journey's best interest in mind. "It would be helpful if you understood this and didn't judge them." Yes, okay, I'd heard this countless times before. Dennis reminded me of that every time I spoke with him.

Cathy went on, "Journey will have to find a safe place to deal with his fear. It would also be really helpful if he felt useful." According to her, he was experiencing a lot of self-loathing because he wasn't working or being productive.

> *I am both bored and fatigued. I am still pretty cheerful considering. It weighs heavy on my heart to be unproductive and weak. I would like to be a force again.*
>
> *~Journey, Summer, 2010*

Cathy then cautioned us before moving on, "I am not a mind reader. Or a psychic. I am sometimes shown the most likely outcome of a given situation, but you must know that a person has free will. Their situation can change. That being said, I do see this as a blip in his life. Not a lifetime sentence."

"But," I stammered, aware that my fear was speaking. I took a couple of deep breaths and told her that the doctors were medicating him against his wishes. "They are setting him on a lifetime course, telling him there is no cure for what he was experiencing. They think that he is sick and can't get well." She replied matter-of-factly, "Just because they believe it, doesn't make it so."

Several days later we received a phone call from a hospital in Marshall, Michigan. Journey was there.

On September 18, 2010, less than 12 hours after

I surrendered Journey to the Infinite Beloved, he'd gotten up at dawn and took a cab to Ann Arbor. He took a cab 70 miles to a hospital he thought could help him. He continued to complain of chest pain, and even though he had stopped talking about it so much, still believed that he had a terminal condition with his colon. University of Michigan has the reputation of being one of the best hospitals nationwide. Unfortunately for Journey, he spent three weeks in their psych ward the year before.

They did not take a chest x-ray or any other diagnostics. Instead, they put his butt in an ambulance and transferred him back to CMH in Ingham County. From there he was taken to the closest open bed which was a hospital in Marshall.

Unlike other psychiatrists, this doctor was willing to speak with us over the phone. Patiently he explained, "people with bipolar often feel better after a while and then stop taking their medication. If he stays on the medication, then perhaps in six months or so, we'll be able to reduce the dose. He'll be just fine if he sticks to the protocol we outline for him. It's important that he eats regular meals, sleeps at night and goes to therapy regularly." I remember thinking that he was probably right but wondered how you forced an adult to do those things.

Since no two doctors thus far had agreed on a diagnosis, I asked this doctor why he thought that Journey had bipolar. "Based on the Minnesota

Multiphasic Personality Inventory (MMPI-2), I've ruled out schizophrenia. He explained, "the MMPI-2, is a psychological test given to help doctors determine a differential diagnosis and a subsequent treatment plan. It consists of 567 multiple choice questions."

"When was Journey given this test?" I inquired. After some shuffling of papers, he answered, "Monday morning, shortly after he arrived."

Journey was taking the 3-hour multiple choice test at the same time we were consulting with the medical intuitive. Perhaps that would explain why Cathy was seeing the random letters; E, A, C, D?

Chapter 29

Out of sight, out of mind, they say. Well I don't blame them for acting how they do. My dad wants to be able to look back on the situation and say he tried his best to save me. I'm sure he would feel guilty his whole life if he thought he neglected to inform me of how to stay healthy. He has, after all, spent most of his life thinking about it. Mom just needs to cry every now and again. She acts how I would if I didn't write.
~ Journey, Summer, 2010

Journey was discharged to Bridges, which is a step-down unit at the CMH building. Often when a patient is discharged from the hospital they go to a freestanding unit for a while before going home. Patients can come and go as they please if they are back by 8 or 9 PM. This allows the staff to make sure the residents have their medication in the morning and in the evening, with complete freedom in between.

The staff was friendly and seemed to be fond of Journey. We were told on numerous occasions that he was considerate of others and often lightened things up. While that may have been true, he still had a mind of his own. After three weeks of being there, just before he was to be discharged, Journey decided to decline his medication. The state laws contend that a person can be forced into treatment if they are a danger to themselves or others. He felt that since he was not a danger to himself and certainly not to others then he shouldn't be forced to take the medication. He complained that he couldn't put two thoughts together and his vision was so blurry he couldn't read even if his mind would cooperate. According to him, the medication rendered him numb and dumb.

I would advocate confining unstable people to a child-proof community, but I find it immoral to drug any person against their will.

~ *Journey, 2010*

Since Journey was not complying with the recommended treatment he was taken by ambulance to yet another hospital. This would be his fifth hospitalization in one year. Journey's "will" was not being tamed as quickly as his doctors had imagined. Much to their dismay, he wasn't learning that he had a "hard-wire" problem, a chemical imbalance, and, like a diabetic, needed daily medication. These doctors were learning for themselves what I had known a lifetime. Journey was as stubborn as a German mule, and force rarely, if ever, worked with him. Journey's noncompliance was costing the state of Michigan and CMH a lot of money and from that perspective he was becoming a pain in the ass.

Arriving at the hospital, Journey again stated the laws as he understood them and insisted upon his own representation. The staff said that they could get a forced court order that mandated medication. Journey said that yes, he was familiar with that form of legal "assistance." He had been through it before. He sat with a doctor in front of a TV monitor and was given little if any room to state his own case. The judge always agreed with the doctor. This time, Journey insisted on his own representation and a trial among his peers. Apparently, since he had enough knowledge of the laws and was cognizant enough to communicate them, for the time being he was detained, but was not forced to take medication.

I remember one sleepless evening at the hospital, the halls were especially empty, and I started playing their piano. I could just feel the place ache with joy. It seemed like angels were singing in the distance. I was so proud, and I

> *looked around, but I couldn't see anyone. I
> could tell that the sound was reaching some-
> one, though. That was the best I ever played the
> piano. Later, I took my comb and hid it inside
> the piano. I wanted to leave some of my identity
> there because I loved it so much.*
>
> ~ *Journey, Summer, 2010*

A couple of weeks into his fifth hospital stay, Rex and I were contacted and asked to consider filing for legal guardianship of Journey. In the meantime, and more specific to the moment, we should "talk some sense" into Journey. If the situation weren't so grim I would have laughed out loud. My mind went to the hundreds of herbal pills we had found in Journey's room after his sudden departure in September.

In the hours of searching for solutions that treat mental illness, I'd come across some encouraging research on a nutraceutical called *bacopa monnieri*. The clinical research, complete with double-blind studies and every other detail that makes research legitimate, took place in India. It involved several hundred patients that had been diagnosed with schizophrenia. Half the patients were given the drug Olanzapine, and the other half were given *nardostachys jatamans* (bacopa monnieri). The results were very promising. In addition to an almost complete reduction of psychotic symptoms, the patients on *bacopa monnieri* had no unpleasant or debilitating side effects.

For several months, we "required" Journey to take the recommended dosage of bacopa. After he left, we found those pills everywhere in his room. Little pills in the chair cushions, in grocery bags stuffed under his bed, in the wastebasket. When confronted, he said that he took them for a few weeks and didn't feel any better. Besides, he insisted, "My head isn't the problem, it's my gut."

So, when this staff person asked me to convince Journey to get on board with medication for life, I was silent. I gathered my thoughts. I told her about the herbal medication and how he hadn't taken the pills. "Well, that's the problem with the mentally ill. They don't know what's best for them in that regard. We have to insist, and if that doesn't work we must force them." I told her that I wished I agreed with her. It would make things so much easier if I believed that pressing him to take medication was the answer. Eventually I confided, "I have a moral issue with forcing Journey to take medication that, at best, masks the symptoms so he's slightly more appealing to be around. The medication does nothing to address the underlying cause of the symptoms. I am looking for a doctor or a treatment that supports true recovery." On a roll, I went on, "Since he is being detained anyway, could you arrange for him to see a therapist that specializes in trauma? And since he'll be forced to take medication, could you force him to take the supplements? I'd be happy to send over the study for the doctor to look at..." I mistook her silence for consideration. I was wrong. Eventually she sputtered, "I have no idea what you're asking. I can't imagine any responsible parent taking your stand." And then remembering her manners, she muttered a hasty "Goodbye" before hanging up on me. I stared at the silent phone in my hand and wondered again why it had to be one way or the other.

Chapter 30

After Journey left with no regard to our concern for him, and then finding the herbal supplements that he agreed to take tucked into various nooks and crannies of his bedroom, we were completely fed up. Perhaps it was time to let the chips fall where they may. It had become glaringly obvious that we could not change Journey's course; not by coercion, logic or pleading. He was an adult and he was making decisions that would impact his life, regardless of our opinions one way or the other. I resolved to back off with my desire to control the outcome. I would do my best to back off, but I knew that I would never give up on his recovery.

~

The good people that believed they knew how to help

Journey became more and more frustrated with his noncompliance. I learned that they were putting off the court trial. One reason is because things in hospitals move as slowly as molasses in December. The other reason we learned by one nurse's nonchalant comment, one that seemed like an afterthought. If Journey was in the hospital a week or so longer, he would exceed the 90-day time limit that constituted short-term care. If a patient cannot be helped within 90 days of short-term care, then it is assumed they can't be helped and need something long-term. Essentially, she told me that the plan was to wait the 10 or so days and then transfer Journey to Michigan's only state mental institution.

I am not sure what images the words "state mental institution" conjure up for most people, but for me, I imagined the sickest people. Vegetative, comatose people that are bedridden, ones with little or no hope of recovering or being discharged. It is not the place for relatively cognitive, albeit frightened, stubborn people that could still carry on an intelligent conversation about their rights.

Yes, I had just made the commitment to back off and let the chips fall and all that, but this was different. I was not going to sit back and let my son be planted in a state institution so that he could be "taught a lesson" in compliance!

That night I couldn't sleep and so I resumed my never-ending search for a person, place or thing that could help my son. In the wee hours of the morning, I must have entered the magic words into the search engine because I found a residential facility in Arizona called The Alternative to Meds Center (ATMC). ATMC is a residential facility that uses orthomolecular medicine along with many other modalities to support mental health issues and to wean people off street drugs or prescription drugs.

At day's first light I put in a call to this facility. Mark, the person in charge of intakes, answered the phone. He explained their program and after hearing my account of Journey's situation felt certain that they could help him. Their recovery rate was impressive.

The intake director assured me that they had worked successfully with hospitals and court-ordered patients before. They could arrange for a bed-to-bed transfer if needed. Their doctors could write a letter to Journey's doctors, or a statement to the judge could be written if that would be useful. I learned that once a patient is there, extensive lab work was done to determine specific deficiencies or if heavy metal toxicity was present. Then a physician and a nutritionist designed an orthomolecular regimen specifically for each patient. The residents participated in gardening, preparing and eating healthy organic food. They had daily group meetings, daily education, and therapy specific to each person's needs twice weekly as well as exercise, saunas, acupuncture and massage. Treatment typically lasted somewhere between 30-90 days. The price tag was daunting, but I knew we would find a way to send him there, even if it meant taking out a second mortgage on our modest home.

I wept with relief. Mark's encouraging reassurance that they could certainly help Journey, the treatment program, the beautiful photographs of their facility, all presented such a stark contrast to the image of the state mental hospital. Time was of the essence and there was a lot of work to do, but I was buoyed by a hope that I hadn't had in a long, long time.

After a couple of phone calls, I was in contact with an attorney who seemed like a good fit. She specialized in collaborative methods and alternative ways to resolve disputes. Her website assured its readers that everyone deserved high-quality legal representation and that she did not believe in a "one size fits all" approach to the law.

An initial conversation with this attorney supported what I already knew; once a person has their guardianship usurped and certainly once they were in a state mental facility, the likelihood of them turning it all around and living a productive life became very slim. She said that a jury trial would tear Journey apart. If she were hired, the first thing she would do would be to advise him to rescind that request. She cautioned that Journey would have to make the call himself to hire her, and if he did, then she would be happy to represent him.

After a visit with Breaha and then Aunt Susan,

Journey made the call to the attorney, and subsequently rescinded his request for a trial. CMH informed him that he had been indecisive before and they were going through with their position. Essentially, they were suing him for guardianship and the right to force treatment. Their plan involved a three-month stay at the state hospital, followed by residency in an adult foster care home where they could make sure he followed treatment.

Back in the early part of the year, during Journey's third or fourth hospitalization, he was required to apply for Medicaid. And although Rex, Journey and I all declined the need for state aid in the form of disability, Journey apparently filled out the Medicaid paperwork, because the week that he hired legal representation, a check came from the state of Michigan. It was several thousand dollars. It included back pay for all the months since he had applied up to that date. The amount was within six dollars of the attorney's fee to represent him.

The next question was where to come up with the money to send Journey to ATMC. Briefly, I considered asking Medicaid to pay for it, but quickly discarded that idea. I had learned many things working at a freestanding birth center and one of them was that insurance companies rarely paid for preventative or alternative medicine. My experience revealed that insurance companies were more interested in putting out fires than preventing them.

My colleagues and I at the birth center were like family. Working day in and day out with women, sometimes up all night at births and into the following day, you get to know them at their worst and their best. These women watched me go from a lively, upbeat woman to one who was often preoccupied, the worry that I felt clear on my face and in my voice. They knew bits and pieces of the ongoing process with Journey but had learned early on that asking me about it at work often resulted in my need to excuse myself to the other room to blow my nose and dab at my eyes. The flipside was if I ever needed a compassionate perspective I could count on any one of them to listen patiently while I processed.

A freestanding birth center was considered "fringy" in conservative Lansing and for the first several years after opening it teetered on the brink of closing more than once. By this time though, in its eighth year, it was mildly profitable. It was the end of the year and supplies were well stocked, bills were all current and there was a tidy sum of money in the bank. I decided to ask for a loan.

I sent out an email asking to move our monthly staff meeting up a week. Getting six busy women together unexpectedly is akin to herding cats, and I took it as a good sign that they all agreed to meet a week early.

Gathered around the table in the birth center's sunny kitchen, five expectant faces looked my way.

I flushed. I have always found it easier to offer help than to ask for it. But, I reminded myself, "This isn't for me. It's for Journey." The depressing images of the state mental hospital propelled me forward. "These women are my friends," I reminded myself. "The worst that can happen is that they say no." I rushed forward, talking way too fast I am sure. I explained the situation with Journey, our hope to send him to Arizona for treatment and the amount of money needed to do so. Even before finishing my "proposal" heads were nodding. "Yes, of course," was the consensus.

It brought to mind an exercise where I was asked to generate a feeling of happiness, anger, sadness or appreciation. I was invited to close my eyes and think of a situation that elicits one of those emotions. For me, the experience that morning at the birth center's kitchen table is now my "go to" situation for appreciation and profound relief. I can generate those feelings of hope in a heartbeat. I will always cherish the gift they gave me that morning. I carry it with me and refer to it frequently when I need a reminder of goodness and generosity.

Chapter 31

On December 15, 2010, Breaha, Rex, Journey's attorney and I all arrived early for Journey's trial. We were ushered into a sterile looking room where fear and apprehension were a part of the very walls and pews. It looked like someone had tried vehemently to polish it away, but the fear remained. Michigan's great seal was predominant on the wall behind the judge's stand. Suddenly it looked ridiculous to me. The stag and elk were on their hind legs and appeared to be dancing. I stifled a nervous laugh. I understood in that moment why people laughed at inopportune times. It is a survival technique of sorts. I felt light-headed and on the edge of falling apart. Laughter seemed more appealing than completely losing it. I stifled both and told myself to pull it together. I dragged my eyes away from the dancing animals and forced them into my lap. I uttered another petition to

God for an outcome that supported Journey's highest good. I forced myself to breathe.

Several moments later, Journey was ushered into the courtroom. Thin as a rail, dark circles under his eyes, he looked frail and frightened. Although Breaha had spent hours searching for the perfect set of clothes that met his very rigid requirements, he was dressed in sweatpants and slippers. His bony wrists were handcuffed behind his back.

Fury churned and rose to form a choking sensation in the back of my throat. The size and weight of the chains and cuffs were disproportionate and looked ridiculous on his pale wrists. This was the person who, as a boy, wept inconsolably when he shot a bird with his BB gun. As far as I knew he hadn't been violent or disrespectful to anyone. I felt Rex's body stiffen next to mine and his hand gripped mine more firmly. I think it was meant to be reassuring to me, but I knew that it was because this scene was equally unbearable for him. Breaha hastily wiped at an errant tear, her face hardening at the injustice of what she saw. Together, almost comically, the three of us took a collective breath and let it out. Sitting directly in front of us, Journey turned and glanced our way. There was the slightest look of amusement on his face. I imagined him saying, "Jeez, you guys. Chill."

Keeping my eyes on the back of Journey's head, I willed him to be courageous. I told him that he was innocent and that we loved him and wouldn't give up on him. Something that Dennis had taught his students umpteen times came to mind, "When in doubt, go to God." I was indeed in doubt. Again, I surrendered Journey and all of his affairs to the Source of all creation. Despite the chill in the room, I saw small beads of sweat forming above Journey's brow. I longed to reach out and wipe them away, tell him it was okay, we had a plan for him, but of course I couldn't. I sat silently waiting to hear what the judge would determine on his behalf.

Journey's attorney gave a brief explanation of the treatment being offered by ATMC, and then a lovely young woman with a kind smile spoke up on behalf of CMH. She informed the judge that CMH was willing to drop the charges if Journey chose the out of state treatment center, and if the family was willing to pay for said treatment. Then the judge spoke to Journey, asking him if he wanted to go to a treatment facility in Arizona. Journey spoke softly, "Yes sir, I would appreciate that opportunity." "What did you say? Speak up, I didn't hear you." In a much louder and clearer voice, Journey repeated, "Yes sir!" This time all four of us took a collective sigh of relief. And that was that. The uniformed guard stood up and Journey was ushered out of the room and back to his police escort. We were advised to pick Journey up at the hospital the following day and have him on a plane within 48 hours.

The following day, Breaha and I met in Owosso to pick Journey up at the hospital. The plan was to stay at Breaha and Zach's home in Midland that night and then meet Rex at the Flint airport in the wee hours of the morning so that the two of them could catch the early flight to Phoenix. Before leaving the hospital, there were hugs and back slapping with several of the other residents, and polite goodbyes to many of the staff. As the last of the paperwork was being signed, one of the nurses approached me to ask about ATMC. I gave a brief explanation per my understanding, including what I had recently learned about ortho-molecular psychiatry.

Someone called the nurse's name and when she turned her attention away briefly, Journey caught my eye and shook his head slightly. On the way out, I asked him why. "I just want to make sure that you are respectful of their way of doing things. I didn't want you to come off as offensive or seem unappreciative for the service that they provided, even if it's not the service we choose." He waited to see if I had a response, but I was speechless. "They are good people Mom. They have a hard job and are doing their best." For a moment, I was like the child in the relationship. Journey had sensed a subtle air of superiority in my voice and he was calling me out.

Journey helped Breaha and Zach prepare dinner that night, but he didn't eat any of it. He feigned nervousness about his upcoming trip. There may have been some truth to that, but it was obvious that this wasn't the first meal he had skipped in a while. There was a light heartedness that felt delicious and I suspect that each of us wanted to savor that feeling.

Journey tended to avoid direct contact with me that night, but he did offer me an awkward hug stating that I was a fierce mama bear and he appreciated it. Good naturedly he bantered with Breaha. Periodically, he would saunter up to her and embrace her in, what over the years had been coined a "head hug." Head hugging was a pseudo hug. It was slightly less intimate and confronting than a true heart to heart hug, but it was affectionate and something that he offered only to Breaha.

The morning was crisp and cold as we said our goodbyes to Breaha and Zach. Not a hint of light shown in the Eastern sky and there was a drizzle of freezing rain coming down. I had a moment's panic as I wondered what would happen if we somehow got detained and didn't make it to the airport. "What if Rex's car broke down? Or he had a flat tire and they missed their flight?"

"Shut up brain!" I scolded myself, "Little self, take a back seat. Look around at the miracles that have played out in the last ten days!"

I forced my shoulders down where they belonged and began to enjoy Journey's company. He told me that he was aware of all of the people that had been praying for him. Many of them, he confessed, he did not know. "I imagine these are your friends. Or perhaps friends of friends?" In any case, he explained, "When I had no hope and wanted to give up, when I thought that I was alone, and my life was worth nothing, I was buoyed by all the love coming my way. I felt like I had to match, with my effort, each person's effort. If they cared enough to hold me in the light, then I had to care enough to keep myself there."

Chapter 32

Someone from ATMC met Rex and Journey at the Phoenix airport. With Journey safely in their care, Rex wondered what he should do next. Should he rent a car and follow them to the center? Would that seem like hovering? He felt Journey was in capable hands, and in the end opted to return home. He wandered around the Phoenix airport for a few hours and then boarded the next flight back to Michigan.

On December 19, just two days after Journey arrived at ATMC, he called home. He said that he felt like he had received a miracle. He was gracious and hopeful. He knew that it was a hardship to send him there, and he would pay us back when he could. He had slept some the night before and had enjoyed some fresh fruit and goat milk yogurt for breakfast. "Hey, maybe the goat milk will heal me, like it did for Heidi. Ha-ha. But seriously, I do feel so much better."

And this was before the lab work was even back? What had happened in that short amount of time? One of the staff members explained to us that Journey had arrived there in a state of psychosis. He was acting like a small child, baby talking and holding his body inward as if to protect himself from some unseen danger. The medical director gave him a large dose of vitamin C along with an even larger dose of vitamin B3 (niacin). So that he wouldn't be fearful, Journey was advised that the vitamin B-3 would cause a major flushing sensation as the small capillaries opened and allowed an increase in blood flow. The director said that within an hour Journey was speaking clearly, shaking hands with the other residents, and getting to know the staff. He was walking upright and carried himself with confidence. I don't know if high doses of Vitamins C and B-3 are enough to cause such a drastic change in someone's physiology or if was the fact that he was surrounded by people who believed he could get well or a combination of both, but we were grateful for the news.

My Christmas gift that year was a call from Journey, "I just woke up from a profound dream!" I couldn't help but marvel that to "wake up from a dream" he must have been sleeping. "Mom, are you listening? I had this lucid dream. It was so cool. I was being held by the love of the world. I know this sounds weird, but I knew that I was loved by everyone and everything. And here is the cool part. I was being held by love, but I was also the one holding the love. Does that make sense? ...It's hard to explain.... well.... anyway, Merry Christmas. And thanks for believing in me."

I couldn't stop smiling that day. My boy was experiencing healing. Later I heard this quote from Saint Francis of Assisi, "What we are looking for is what is looking," and I understood what it meant. I got it. And it sounded like Journey got it, too.

I experienced Sedona through Journey's eyes. Every few days he would call with something new that he had seen or experienced. One day he described the beauty of the red mountains, the next time he explained that Sedona was considered sacred healing grounds by the Natives. In the past, no one had lived there, people would just come from all over to experience healing and then leave, "like us here at the center."About a month into his stay I received a message on my voicemail from him. I saved it on my phone and listened to it over and over so that I could hear his voice happy and hopeful. "Hi Mom. How is everything? I just wanted to tell you that I am getting so much stronger. We go hiking almost every day, and I can hike further each time. I am actually building muscle!"

This was the voice of the son that I knew. Journey continued to recover and as he did he began contemplating his future. One day he rented a car and drove the 30 miles from Sedona to Flagstaff. He toured

Northern Arizona University and imagined it would be a great place to study. He made several calls to U of M, the bank where he held student loans, and eventually to Rex, "I still have perfect credit! Thank you, Dad!" Rex had taken the time and interest to see that Journey's student loans were in deferment and had been making payments toward the interest. Journey's affairs were in order so that when he was ready, he could move forward with his life, credit intact.

Journey imagined himself staying in Arizona. Sedona reminded him of a smaller version of Ann Arbor. The idea of a fresh start was appealing. This was what we wanted for Journey, so we were pleased that he had a vision for his future. Journey got a loan, bought a car, and began looking for a job and a place to live.

Chapter 33

After his 90-day stay, the owner of ATMC offered Journey an internship. We were thrilled at the opportunity and then disappointed when Journey said that he felt ready to move away from their protective eye. He was applying for jobs downtown and at the mall. He needed a part-time job for just six months until school started in the fall.

He found a temporary place to stay, a beautiful unfurnished loft apartment. He rented it for one month in hopes of finding something more permanent. The good folks at ATMC brought by a twin mattress for him to borrow and he had a tea kettle and cup. Besides that, he had large open windows through which the sun shone in bright rays across the polished wood floors.

"Everything would be perfect if only I had my guitar. God, I miss playing. Would you be willing to send it along with a few other things to set up house?" Journey requested. I went to Marshall's, bought a pan and some utensils and wrapped them along with some second-hand dishes into bedding and towels. I added the meager collection of clothing that he owned and sent it all along with his guitar to Sedona. He shopped for a car and secured a loan from a family member. From that perspective, it seemed that Journey was on his way to the bright future we had always imagined for him.

Jobs weren't plentiful and after three weeks of searching, Journey had yet to land one. He was reluctant to sign a lease on an apartment without a job and so at least to us, it began to look like he may be coming back to Michigan. That, of course, would have been the logical move. Either that or go back to ATMC and accept the internship that they had offered. Instead, enthusiastic about having his "life back" Journey had reconnected with friends on Facebook. One friend from high school lived in San Francisco and invited him to come to California and stay with him for a while. This friend worked at Google and was taking classes at the local college. He told Journey that he could use some help with his calculus.

Journey didn't ask for our opinion and resisted when I offered it anyway. I had a bad feeling about him making that move and I told him so. "Mom, I have no friends left in Lansing. David has room for me and may be able to help me find a job." San Francisco seemed much more appealing than Lansing. I got it, but I didn't like it.

Packing his car with his meager belongings, Journey drove west.

We learned from the staff at ATMC that he had declined buying a three-month supply of the supplements that they recommended. One component at ATMC was education. They taught the residents that it was important to stay on the supplemental regimen for at least one year and, depending on the propensity and the illness, some people take them for the rest of their lives. Our son left the facility without a care in the world and without the supplements that had helped bring him back into balance. Journey, the person who was described as a "young adult male with above average intelligence" was behaving like he had none.

Before he made it to David's, the transmission went out on the car that he had just purchased. Furthermore, the "space" that David had for Journey was a small patch of floor to sleep on. David and his friends liked to party.

After the initial phone call telling us that he had made it to San Francisco and the unfortunate news about his car, we didn't hear from him for days. He would respond to texts but not our phone calls. "Oh, God, not this again." I thought to myself. In the past, Journey would avoid direct contact with us when he wasn't clear. Intuitively I knew that he wasn't doing well. The stress of having borrowed money for a now useless car, not eating a balanced diet, no bed to sleep in, and probably using drugs and alcohol were all detrimental to his recent recovery. Anxiety rose and threatened my newfound peace of mind. I was furious. I used that anger as a drug to anesthetize myself from that hard rock of fear that threatened to take up residency once again in my gut.

Almost as if on cue, I was given a personal wake up call. During those days when Journey had once again fallen off our radar, I had a telling dream: I was in a church-like setting. The stained-glass windows shone beautiful green and blue light on my face, my hands and the immediate area around me. I remember turning my face toward it like a blossom seeking the sun that it craves. I was being instructed, but by whom I did not know. There was a voice, neither masculine nor feminine and with no form. Kind of like Oz behind the curtain, except there was no curtain and the voice wasn't corny and booming like in the film.

Seemingly I was alone in this beautiful setting which had changed, as dreams often do, to a sunny patch of earth outside. In a no-nonsense way, I learned that I was at a fork in the road in my life. I had been ignoring my own health and needs for too long. My constitution was strong, but a person isn't meant to be functioning in crisis mode constantly. I was told that in a couple of years everyone that I was worried about would be "past the crisis point" and if I didn't do something to manage my stress I would be the next one in crisis. I was left with a question, "When there is no one else to worry about, do you want to be healthy and free to enjoy that, or do you want to be the one who needs to be taken care of?"

I woke up with a start, the dream echoing in my mind. Some dreams are simply random images that have little or no meaning. They are wispy and flee as soon as we wake from them. Other dreams leave us with an emotional jolt. Not only do we remember them upon awakening, but they show up unbidden by us throughout the day, complete with the emotional imprint that came with them. Such was the case with this dream.

I knew that I had been pushing myself. I intended to get back to yoga class, eat more fresh food, meditate more often. I just didn't have time right then, I told myself. Not only was Journey's life in apparent turmoil, my sister Lana had received a recent diagnosis of Lou Gehrig's disease and needed constant care. Between staying overnight with her a couple of nights per week, worrying about my mom as she prepared to watch her second daughter die, and the constant worry about Journey, I figured I would focus on my health "later" when I had more time.

I wish that I was the type of person who dealt with their stress by walking hours per day, or lifting weights at the gym, or like a friend of mine who scrubs her house from top to bottom and then starts over again. I dealt with my stress by being physically helpful if possible, researching everything I could find on a given topic, and even though I knew better, worrying incessantly. Although my physician friends assured me that a little pill for anxiety could be very helpful, my drug of choice was one American Spirit cigarette and a soak in the hot tub at the end of the day.

I knew intellectually that I was Love, that Journey and Lana were Love and that we are eternal, spiritual beings learning lessons that would bring us closer to self-realization. I also knew that I was a spiritual being living in a self-induced hell and my time of denial had come to an end.

It was then that I dug out the "reality management worksheet," a profound step-by-step process that takes a person through the ancient process of forgiveness. By forgiveness, I mean the original Aramaic definition of cancelling or removing something inside of us that doesn't belong, not today's distorted version of letting someone else off the hook. I had learned this process years ago and experienced profound healing and true change in my perception. Unfortunately, I had failed to realize that it was a lifetime process. I sort of felt like I had "done the work." But this time, I realized if we are in bodies, the "work" is never done. It is an ongoing process of cleaning up our stores so that we are creating from Love instead of our fear and hostility. So, although my life still resembled a living hell, slowly, day by day, with the practice of forgiveness, it was becoming more bearable.

Chapter 34

A couple of weeks after Journey arrived in California, Rex received a phone call from an ER physician at a San Francisco hospital. Journey had been brought to their facility after a manager at a local Target store had called the police. Journey had been wandering around the store with no shoes on, no shopping cart and apparently, no intention of leaving any time soon. Journey told the police and the ER physician that he had an airline ticket for a return trip to Michigan in two days' time. Journey spoke with Rex, told him his flight information and asked if he could borrow a bit of money for a hotel stay until his flight left. Between Rex and the ER doctor, they found a hotel near the airport, paid for it over the phone, called a cab to take Journey there, and because the doctor was a person that truly cared about people, he gave Journey some cash for food. When Rex asked for his address to repay him, the doctor simply replied, "No need for that. I am happy to help."

Two days later at the appointed time, Rex was at the Detroit airport waiting in the terminal where Journey's plane was to land. Eventually Rex spotted him slowly making his way down the corridor. Journey had shoes on, but other than a backpack, was empty handed. He had sold his $2,000.00 guitar for $800.00 and then lost that money gambling at a casino.

Rex greeted Journey warmly and encouraged him to get into the car. He refused. Instead, Journey insisted that Rex reveal his identification. "How do I know you're who you say you are?" Exasperated, Rex drew out his driver's license. "Oh sorry, Rex, I didn't recognize you. The thing is…. I told you that I was flying back to Michigan today, but I never asked you to pick me up."

No amount of kindness, logic or cajoling, softly or firmly, convinced Journey to get in the car. When Rex reminded him that he was penniless and alone at the Detroit airport, Journey assured him that he was resourceful. He had no intention of getting in his dad's car and he was beginning to feel harassed. Rex resorted to finally begging him, pleading with him to get into the car, but Journey refused and walked away. Rex left the airport, got five minutes away and went back. Circling around and around the airport, he couldn't find Journey anywhere.

Rex was crying so hard that he had to pull the car off the road to call and tell me that he didn't have Journey with him. He vacillated between sobbing and cursing as he explained to me what had happened. In my anger, I wanted to make Rex responsible, "What? You couldn't just make him get in the car?" But I knew better than anyone, that if Journey refused, he meant it. I thought back to the months while living with us when he would not eat anything but carbohydrates. If he saw one glistening drop of fat floating on his soup, he would vehemently push it away, even as his stomach growled in earnest. I knew that Rex had done all he could. If Journey refused to get into the car, there was no making him do it.

This is where, if it were possible to turn down my "give a shit" meter, I would have. I wanted to care less, I just didn't know how to make that happen. As though I thought God might be deaf or dumb, I asked on a regular basis what I should be doing to help my son. This time I heard that I should "make my home within the breath," whatever that meant. In all the times I'd asked, I never heard that I should harden my heart.

Rex and I held each other closely those days, literally and figuratively. We consoled ourselves by saying that Journey had experienced a healing and that he knew how he got there. He knew with certainty that he was loved and that he had a home to return to should he choose. It was all that we could do.

Chapter 35

A few weeks later there was a "Journey spotting" in Ann Arbor. A family friend's daughter worked at a coffee shop there and told her parents that she thought she recognized him. While preparing his latte, she spoke up, "Hey, don't I know you? Aren't you Journey?" a brief look of surprise crossed his face. He told her that his name was Shay. And this wasn't totally false. Shay is his middle name. Obviously, he didn't want to be recognized. He didn't return to that coffee shop, at least not while she was working.

I was relieved that he was alive and on the heels of that relief was anger. His apparent disregard for his family was hard to comprehend. How could our son, who knew inside and out that he was cherished, the child who shared with me a private joke about being created from the same batch of cookie dough, not care that I was sleepless with worry most nights?

That when I did finally nod off, I prayed for him even in my sleep? The fact that his mind was murky mollified my intellect but did nothing for my aching heart. His apparent indifference provided me with a plethora of subject matter for my "reality management worksheets."

A few days later, we woke up to find that we had a missed call with an Ann Arbor area code, but there was no message. Flustered, I wondered how it was possible to have missed the call. Absentmindedly, I held the painful knot in my gut, trying not to hover over Rex as he redialed the number. Almost immediately, I learned that he was talking to someone at the Ann Arbor police station. An officer informed Rex that a few weeks ago Journey had been seen showering at a residence hall on campus where he obviously didn't live. The students reported it to the Resident Advisor who confronted Journey and asked him not to come back. Apparently, surviving as a homeless vagabond on the University of Michigan campus was Journey's idea of being resourceful.

Ignoring the advisor's appeal, he was there again, this time sleeping under the stairs. The resident advisor called the police. I imagined my son, curled up in a tight ball, cold and lonely under a dirty stairwell and wondered how he had gotten to that place. We were living in a bad dream. Not for the first time, I wondered if it felt this miserable for me, how it must be for Journey.

A gentle prod from the tip of the officer's baton had Journey on his feet in one movement. Already in a semi-crouch, he didn't have far to reach to swoop up his backpack. He told the officer that he was just about to leave. The officer offered to give him a ride, but it soon became evident that he had nowhere to go. After some encouragement, Journey finally gave him our home phone number. When we didn't answer the phone, the officer asked him if there was someone else who could vouch for him. Journey provided a home phone number to one of his childhood friends, one of the few phone numbers that he had committed to memory. This man had become a family friend over the years and cared deeply for Journey. He is a responsible citizen that works as a social worker in Lansing and felt obligated to tell the police about Journey's mental health history. By the time we learned all of this, Journey had already been taken from the police station to the hospital.

My heart went out to him. I couldn't help it. I was filled with sorrow. He was back in the system that we had tried so hard to keep him out of. My sorrow felt a lot like pity and I was reminded of a conversation that I had with Journey the summer before. After acting like a colossal jerk, especially when his friends were around, I had asked him why he was being so mean to people who were trying to reach out to him. Tears welled up in his eyes and he walked away. Later he came back, "You want to know why I act like a jerk? Because I would 100 times rather be feared than pitied! I can't stand the thought of my friends pitying me, okay?" I knew that under the tough guy façade was a frightened, prideful young man trying to come to terms with a world that he could no longer trust or navigate.

> *Why did my body break? No doctor has told me. I will probably never know what specifically went wrong and why. All I know is that I am out of the race. I am no longer a person to strive to be better than. I am someone to pity. I am someone to feel sorry for. What a waste of time. I'd rather not exist than be pitiful.*
>
> *~Journey, Summer, 2010*

Chapter 36

If I had any unconscious smugness about Journey leaving Owosso Memorial Hospital, it was gone. Now, all I felt was humility. I was grateful for Journey's sake that he had been polite albeit stubborn while there before. They went through the process again of court-ordered treatment. This time Journey acquiesced. The court order was for one year.

From the moment Journey was born, and while watching him grow, teachers, friends and family couldn't wait to see what this funny, brilliant, quirky kid would become. He had always had a competitive streak and I knew much of that pressure was self-inflicted. But, now I wondered if it had been a mistake to tell him he was brilliant and could do anything he set his mind to. Perhaps we should have given him a more traditional upbringing. Maybe it was too much pressure to tell a child that God existed within all of creation including him.

Journey refused our attempts to visit. He told us in a note that it was too stressful on all of us for him to come home. He put out feelers for another place to stay, sometimes hinting, and a few times directly asking family members or close friends if he could stay with them for a while. I know it was hard for him to ask and being told "no" added to his own self-loathing. I hoped that someone would be willing to take him in, and I also understood why people wouldn't or couldn't.

A few weeks later when Journey was discharged, Breaha and Zach picked him up and took him to their house. He talked of his regrets of going to California, how he had experienced success at ATMC and had thrown it away. "You can't imagine how it feels being on this mind-numbing medication. I can't conjure a clear thought. I feel like a ghost of myself. My vision is blurry, and I am nauseated all the time. At ATMC there are a lot of rules and a shitload of pills to swallow, but at least I can think a thought and eat a meal. At least I am still me."

The fact is, if we had the money we would have sent Journey back to ATMC in a heartbeat. We lived modestly, in the same home we had lived in for the past 30 years. Rex and I both worked hard but basically lived with a few months' savings in reserve. Rex had an elderly family member who'd worked hard, invested well and consequently had a comfortable nest egg. She had implied over the years that there may be an inheritance left for Rex when she died. We knew that we absolutely could not in good conscience borrow more money, but I did wonder if this aunt would be willing to part with Rex's inheritance early to invest in Journey's recovery. Rex was reluctant to ask her, but eventually did, because like me, he wanted Journey to have every opportunity to get well.

After a day or two of consideration, Rex's aunt agreed to give him his inheritance money early. That, along with a very generous monetary gift from a friend, allowed us to send Journey back to ATMC.

The entire family sat around the dinner table and had a "Come to Jesus" meeting. Journey, sincere in his desire to go back, thanked us profusely for the taking that money and investing in him...again. "When I am well and have a good paying job, I will pay you guys back. Okay?" We got creative and came up with a working plan that covered the following year. And most importantly, we extracted a promise from Journey to see it through.

While we were convinced that ATMC had a viable model for recovery, we were also sure that until Journey dealt with some deeper core issues, he could not experience true freedom.

Our friends, Michael and Jeanie Ryce have a healing center called Heartland in the Ozark Mountains in Missouri. Michael is the author of the book, *Why is this Happening to Me....Again!?* as well as the *Reality*

Management Worksheet. Both were works that Rex and I knew from personal experience to be profound life-changers.

Heartland has a work-study program where interested people can stay on the land, work on the property 8 hours a day, and in exchange, their food and lodging are covered. Additionally, they can participate in the intensive workshops taught at Heartland every summer.

Our plan was for Journey to spend 90 days at ATMC, and the following nine months at Heartland. In our opinion, those two programs combined would be the best possible chance Journey had for true and full recovery. We were excited for this possibility and made the necessary plans to get Journey to ATMC for the second time that year.

With Journey back at the Sedona center, in the capable hands of the doctors and staff there, the rest of us decided to go ahead with our family plans for a much-needed vacation. We packed up a few things and moved into a rented lake house with a dock that extended out into the cool, crisp water of Lake Michigan. After all the stress and tension, this place felt like a slice of heaven.

Chapter 37

Two days into our vacation and less than a week at ATMC Journey called. He said that it was a mistake to spend all that money for him to be there. "I should just come home. It's not too late to get your money back." Our heads were spinning! "What are you talking about Journey?!"

"I don't need to be here. Really. It was a mistake and a waste of your money. I don't need to be here to come off the medication..."

"Journey, wait. What happened? Where is this coming from?"

We patiently reminded him that going off the medication on his own hadn't worked in the past, and that a court order existed in Michigan that he comply with treatment. We reminded him, less patiently, of the promise he made to follow through.

I was pissed. We all were. Despite all that we had

done for him, he still had the audacity to act as though his whims were superior to any logical thought. After the third call, I told him firmly, "Journey, you are where you need to be and where you agreed to be. Focus on yourself and your recovery. If you leave before the 90 days are up, you are on your own." We all turned off our phones and did our best to enjoy the rest of our vacation.

While it was true that Journey needed to be in treatment, it was also true that I needed a respite from the constant angst. I didn't realize until he was back at ATMC, how much I needed that hiatus. The reality is, mental illness takes a tremendous toll on everyone in a family, and ours was no exception.

Once I began to relax, it became evident how much I had been consumed by worry and fear. And while I knew that fear compromises one's intelligence, and I had been functioning from that compromised place for too long, I couldn't seem to stop. All of those sleepless nights imagining the worst-case scenarios, had me on what felt like a train moving lickety split toward an unwelcome destination.

I often use the metaphor of a moving train when I am talking to my clients about childbirth. "Early labor is like a train sitting at the station. The engine is rumbling, but the train isn't moving. Slowly, as the train begins to move down the track, it gains momentum. I tell them, like the moving train, their labor is less likely to stall out as it progresses and gains momentum. For pregnant women, this analogy makes sense and helps them understand the value of waiting for active labor to kick in before going to the hospital. For me, that summer, I realized that the train of fear and worry had gained a lot of momentum, and while I knew I had to get a grip, it was like trying to turn the titanic on a dime.

Four weeks after our vacation, the doctor at the center reported that Journey was cognizant and appeared to be clear headed. There were no psychotic episodes as they weaned him from pharmaceutical medication to the nutraceutical supplements. "If I had just met Journey and did an evaluation, I would not be able to diagnose him with mental illness." He went on to tell us that Journey participated in the daily education sessions, the required group activities, therapy twice per week and the food and nutritional supplements. "He's putting up quite a stink about the daily sauna sessions, but other than that, he is doing exceptionally well."

Journey called home regularly to complain about the saunas. "I feel good until I do the saunas and then I feel nauseated and utterly depleted. Forty-five minutes in a far infrared sauna burns 500 calories," he lamented. "I don't have any extra weight to lose!"

We spoke with him almost daily encouraging him to stick with it, as it was a required part of the treatment. Detoxing was considered an important part of the daily regime at ATMC. Personally, I didn't think

Journey's psychosis was related to heavy metal toxicity, or any toxicity for that matter. He was raised on organic food long before that was a thing, he drank purified water his whole life and never had tooth decay or mercury fillings. I conveyed this to the program director and although he understood, he still insisted that Journey participate.

Six weeks into the three-month program, Journey simply refused to continue the sweats. Angrily, he said that he was tired of being told what to do. "Everyone acts like they know what is best for me! No one listens to me and what I know about myself!" We had heard from previous therapists that people who survive violence often go to extremes to have a modicum of control in their lives. We also knew that Journey was shrewd and could talk a homeless man out of his last dime.

While he was at it, he informed us that he knew with certainty he could not work 40 hours a week of physical labor at Heartland. He doubted he could work 20 hours. "Besides, Michael and Jeanie are leaving in November. I will be there all winter practically by myself. Well, with a handful of old geezers that run the place!" I rolled my eyes and sat down hard. God, I was exhausted. Where was the cheerful and hopeful son that left ATMC just a few months prior?

It was true that Michael and Jeanie taught on the road nine months out of the year. I thought of Journey being one of a handful of people at Heartland...and

I vacillated. It was another turning point, but I didn't see it at the time. I wish that I could say that we had said "Tough. Go work it out. You can't come home until next year." But we didn't. We weren't prepared to put Journey on the street and he knew it. So, while we acquiesced about the stay at Heartland, we were adamant that he finish the 90 day treatment at ATMC.

That last month, we were in constant dialogue with the activity director. "I am sorry, but we can't have participants refusing any part of the treatment. We have done all we can to help Journey, but since he isn't being compliant, it's time for him to leave." We understood their stand, but we were also not willing to back down. We told him again that Journey could not come home one day before he completed treatment. "Is there something Journey can do in leu of the saunas? Is there any way he can stay and complete the 90 treatment? He really needs to do that before he can come home…"

Apparently, there wasn't, because on day 73, Journey called to tell us he was being discharged the following day and that he would be home soon. We told him (again!) that he could not come home. Period.

So, to his credit, he contacted Michael and arranged for a two week stay at Heartland. There was a small refund for his "early departure" (i.e. being kicked out of ATMC) and that was just enough to cover his stay at Heartland as a non-work-study participant.

Michael had several requirements of Journey while he was there. For the entire fifteen days, he was required to watch five hours of instruction per day, turn in written notes illustrating that he understood the material and do five *Reality Management Worksheets* every day. On the home front, Rex and I were watching the same video instruction and doing our own five forgiveness worksheets per day. Although we had let ourselves be bamboozled by Journey's cunning ways, I still felt hopeful.

If Journey had participated with any amount of earnestness, if it had been his own idea, I know with certainty that he would have derived lasting benefit. As it was, he was there in physical body only, going through the motions to fulfill a commitment, simply biding his time until he came home.

Chapter 38

Journey arrived home in mid-October, on day 91, in good spirits. He had a handful of supplements with him but was indignant when I tried to ask him about them. He staked out a little corner for himself on the living room couch, set up his laptop, and pretty much hung out there during his waking hours. If he were to receive a diagnosis at that time, it would have simply been "laziness." I felt exhausted from trying to change his course. I told myself to go with the flow. I reminded myself that my job was to be patient and practice trust. Somewhere along the way, I had developed the idea that four years was significant. I am not sure why, or what I thought really, but in my mind, I would think "in another year or two, things will be different. This is just a blip in Journey's life. He will get better and move on."

This world is fragile, and every year that passes brings you closer to the day that you or someone you love will die. You can tragically blame them for it, or you could be a grownup and understand that the circle of life has greater power than any person, or all of humanity combined.
                                                    ~*Journey, Autumn, 2010*

My sister, Lana's illness was progressing, and her need of full-time care fell to one hired worker, the hospice nurse, me and my mom. Between my trips to her apartment on my lunch hours and spending one or two nights per week, I didn't perseverate on Journey quite as much. I am sure that was a welcomed relief all the way around.

That Thanksgiving, Lana's only child died. At 37 years old, she died unexpectedly from undiagnosed pneumonia. Lana was already dependent on a feeding tube and could barely ambulate from one chair to the next. She had lost her will to live and I knew that our time together was ending.

Journey expressed sadness, mostly for me, my mom and our loss. He did his best to cheer me up reading funny quips that he found, or by engaging in lively conversations whenever I was home and up to it. He asked to go visit Aunt Lana and confirmed what I thought, "She looks wispy and I am not talking about her body. Her life force is waning. It's sad that you have had so many losses." He put his arms around me in a brief and awkward hug. "Sorry, Mom."

That Christmas was low-key. We celebrated quietly at home and we were grateful to have Journey with us. He bought everyone gifts that he thought we would enjoy and seemed more himself than he had in a while.

Chapter 39

They say there are no guidebooks about parenting and there certainly aren't any about dying. Maybe watching someone you are close to die would help.

~Journey, Autumn, 2010

The day after Christmas, my sister Lana called and said that she couldn't get out of bed to use the commode that sat two feet away. She was ready to go to hospice. I was her durable power of attorney and knew that when she went into hospice she was not going there to live, she was going there to die.

We had discussed this before. Mom would not be there for this part of Lana's journey; Lana did not want Mom to see her leave home for the last time. I rode with her in the ambulance to the Eaton Community Palliative Care. I watched as they tucked her into a comfy bed, the downy comforter fluffed around her. I took my job seriously and informed the staff of her wishes to be sedated so that she wasn't in pain. "Also, no food or water through the feeding tube," I dutifully intoned. "Yes, we have all of that written right here. We will make her comfortable." I kissed Lana goodbye and told her that I would be back in the morning.

In case you don't know, "sedated so as not to feel pain" is a euphemism for knocked unconscious. I should have known this, but I didn't. I did not know that I had seen her beautiful smile for the last time. Somehow, I thought that she would float in and out of conscious awareness until she finally died, but I was wrong. The next day, and every day after, when I went to see her she was in a deep sleep.

When I got home I closed myself in my bedroom and cried into my pillow. To no one in particular, I said, "I should have known what 'sedated' meant. But I didn't. If I had known I would have done something...or said something..." My lament trailed off. I knew that there was nothing left to do or say. Lana and I had spent many hours talking about life and death. We had said everything that needed to be said. It's just that I thought I would see her awake again. She had beautiful gray-green eyes. I didn't know that I had seen them for the last time.

Five days later, on New Year's Eve, Mom and I arrived at the hospice center. We were told based on

Lana's vitals she wasn't expected to live through the next 24 hours. My mom had confessed to both Lana and I that she couldn't bear to be present when Lana died. Nevertheless, that night, she couldn't dream of leaving the building.

The hospice house was always full of food. Steaming trays of yummy smelling comfort food were available for every meal. Sitting around the table with strangers putting on their bravest faces wasn't going to work that evening, no matter how much butter was in the mashed potatoes. I told Mom that I was hungry for steak, and somehow, she believed me. There was one daughter left to feed, by God, and she was going to feed her!

Driving into the small town of Charlotte, we eventually made our way to the only restaurant that serves both steak and booze. I introduced my mom to the cosmopolitan. "Well that sure is a little glass," my mom said as she took a big slurp. "Whew, that's tasty," she took another drink and sat the martini glass down. "And kind of strong, too."

My mom is blessed with lots of friends and most of them had been visiting the hospice house all week. They meant well of course, but Mom was exhausted and not sleeping much at all. Those drinks were medicinal. Pure and simple.

As the waitress brought our food, my mom complimented her on her hair. The overweight and slightly frumpy-looking woman beamed. I marveled at my mom's ability to brighten a complete stranger's day, even when her own was so bleak.

I snuck a look at my watch. It was five thirty in the afternoon, barely dark outside and way too early for people to be out celebrating the coming of a new year. I knew that it was out of my control if Lana died while we were gone. I had promised her that I would be there, God willing, and I took that promise to heart. I had one Cosmo and Mom had two. We drank our drinks, made small talk and pushed uneaten food around on our plates.

Back at the hospice house I led my mom into the little den with the overstuffed sofa. I tucked a pillow under her head and before I had the second blanket over her, her eyes were closed, her breathing heavy.

I told Lana to scoot over so that I could get in bed with her. Of course, she didn't move. She hadn't moved all week. I maneuvered her body, heavy with morphine, into my arms and smoothed back her hair. I told her that she had worked so hard with no complaints and we were all so proud of her. I sang off key. I emphasized the large collection of family members that had gone before her and declared that she would have the best Welcome Home party ever. I asked her to "give me a sign" from the other side if she were able. I reminded her how much she was loved.

It wasn't long before Lana's breathing wasn't really breathing. The breaths were shallow and halting and her lungs sounded wet as her body attempted to pull air into them. I assured her that there were so many people praying for her, so much love for her. I invited her to take all that love and use it as a bridge to go home.

And then a remarkable thing happened. My sister's eyes opened, and she looked at me. There was such a look of wonder and awe in them that I knew she must be seeing a slice of heaven. I breathed softly "Yes, that's right Sis, go home." Joy flooded through my body and for a split-second I felt the wonder of what awaits us on the other side. With one last exhale, her eyes closed again, and I knew that her soul was gone.

Chapter 40

As winter turned to spring, Journey began spending his days in East Lansing. Almost every day, as soon as he was out of bed, he would walk to the bus stop and be gone until the last bus dropped him off in the evening. He hung out in the bookstores and coffee shops where other young people were. He seemed to be finding his way. It had been nine months since he had been medicated and he wasn't symptomatic; at least not outwardly. I dared again to hope that he was on the other side of this nightmare.

Journey came home one day in late April, "You know those friends that I met recently? I think I mentioned them to you. Anyway, they need someone to help with their rent over the summer. I am going to move into their place with them next week." I thought, "Those friends you met? The ones we *haven't* met? Haven't even heard about?" I began to voice these thoughts, but Journey was already on his way out the door. Once again, he wasn't asking. He was informing.

Like I said, we had never met these people, but Journey trusted them. He trusted one of them enough to give him his EBT card to buy some food. When Journey asked for it back, the guy refused. The two of them had words, but still the "friend" would not return the card. I don't know who threw the first punch or if it was the only punch, but Journey ended up with an injured spleen.

We were blissfully ignorant of this, however, until Journey called us from the hospital. The regular hospital, not the psych hospital. He sounded almost proud. After the fight and his lost EBT card and money, Journey went to the Volunteers of America. He had been sleeping on a cot there for a couple of days when one of the staff questioned him about the obvious pain he was in. The staff person at the VOA encouraged Journey to get it checked out. The Emergency Room doctor was concerned enough to admit him. He wanted to run some tests and keep him a few days for observation.

On the second day of his hospital stay, Journey called and asked Rex to go to the Volunteers of America and pick up his phone. "And Dad, do you think that I could, you know…come home when I get discharged?" I was ashamed of my skepticism, but I wondered if he would get discharged or simply be moved to the Behavior Health campus. I figured this would be a good test to see if Journey was still relatively clear-headed. If he was inclined toward psychosis, any trained doctor would know it and act.

On the third day, Journey was discharged and came home.

Chapter 41

All that spring and summer I was getting this internal nudge to take some time for myself. "Ha!" I thought, "Not likely." As a doula, I was always on call and I had my job at the birth center. This intuitive whisper was persistent though. There was something that I had to do, and I had to do it alone. "I heard you," I would hiss to myself. "I just don't see how." The "small, still voice" that I had been trying to cultivate was beginning to sound bossy. I did my best to eke out an hour or two when I could, but for the most part life was barreling forward, and I patted myself on the back for remembering to breathe.

Journey's yearlong court order was due to be dropped or renewed in July. His caseworker at CMH continued to be a breath of fresh air. She was young enough, I guess, to still have hope for people. She had a big heart and advocated for Journey just about as much as we did. During a phone conversation she told me, "I didn't have the pleasure of knowing Journey before he was diagnosed, so when he called me from the treatment center in Arizona I was amazed and delighted at his insight and clarity. It was lovely to meet a more accurate depiction of the young man named Journey."

Since he hadn't had any recent episodes, she informed Journey that she was going to recommend dropping the court order. He was free to go about his life as he saw fit. He came home lighthearted and asked me if I would help him clear his name. He didn't like that every time he went to a doctor; mental illness was the first thing that they saw.

Shortly after the court order was lifted, Journey began having sleepless nights. I made several recommendations including the Reality Management worksheets, and over-the-counter sleep remedies. He laughed even though I hadn't made a joke. I continued to feel the remarkable clearing in my own mental and emotional state and knew that Journey would see the changes too. He would see the changes in me and maybe benefit through osmosis. After two nights of no sleep I suggested getting a prescription for pharmaceutical medication knowing that sleep was crucial to maintaining the fragile balance between sanity and madness. He shrugged nonchalantly and walked away.

My heart sank one day when I came home to find

that Journey had gone through several photo albums. There was a pile of confetti made from family photos. Journey suspected that part of his soul had been trapped in the pictures. I was sad, of course, to have lost the one thing that I would save in a fire, my photos. But I was much sadder to know that Journey was struggling again. I assured him that his soul resided in his body and in the presence of Love. He wasn't convinced, so I took the rest of the photos and small mementos from his childhood and hid them safely away in the birth center basement.

I made Journey an appointment with a local physician who agreed to see him, order some of the supplements he had been taking at ATMC and oversee their use. Journey agreed to go, albeit reluctantly. The morning of his appointment, I saw him go into his bedroom and then a few minutes later, text me asking for the address of the doctor's office. I gave him the information and then texted back, "Do you want a ride? I am happy to take you. Your appointment is in 20 minutes." "No" he texted back, "I am on the bus." Oh, dear God. How many times had we asked Journey not to use his bedroom window as a door? Irreverent of our wishes, he had blatantly ignored us and done it anyway.

That evening, as dinner finished simmering, I went downstairs to retrieve a beverage. Coming back up the stairs, I saw Journey marching outside through the backyard with, the pan held in front of him like it contained a bomb. "Hey!" I shouted, just as he dumped the whole thing into the compost. "That's our dinner! What do you think you are doing?" He stomped in, slammed the cast iron skillet back on the stove and looked at me sternly, "You shouldn't cook food in that pan. It is toxic. That food would have killed you!"

Journey began throwing things away; perfectly good things. Not giving them away but dumping them in the trash. We reminded him of the people at Volunteers of America and their need of clothing and music and backpacks. We told him that his Garmin was unused and if he didn't want it, it could be sold for a small sum of money. He didn't listen. He made regular trips to the dumpster until eventually Rex put his foot down.

Journey had given away everything he owned except a handful of clothing and his phone. We sat him down (figuratively since he wouldn't sit down) and reminded him of the freedom we had given him. We told him that there were a few things that were deal breakers. He would have to respect our property. He could not throw away our belongings or destroy our photographs. And no more climbing out of his window. He had to use the door like everyone else. He shrugged his shoulders, which was typical those days, and walked away.

Chapter 42

Rex and I were interested in the workshop, *Why is this Happening to Me...Again!?* that was being offered at Heartland in August. We asked Journey to join us, but he refused. We were reluctant to leave Journey at home, but also knew that doing our own inner work was the best possible thing we could do for ourselves and for Journey.

Breaha and Zach invited him to come up to Midland, but he refused their offer. We decided to invite a male family friend to stay at our home, sleep downstairs in the healing room, and take care of the garden, the house plants and the dog. Journey balked at the idea, "Why don't you trust me to stay home alone? I'm an adult and I don't need one of your nerdy friends babysitting me. Rex tried reason, "Son, you barely speak to us these days. You have little interest in the dog and even less in gardening. This friend has agreed to do some outdoor projects for me, and this will give him the opportunity to work on them." Journey walked away without a word. We mistakenly took his silence for compliance.

We left for the Ozarks on a Friday morning and our friend was scheduled to arrive on Saturday. When he knocked on the door, Journey refused to let him in the house. On the phone, Journey sounded panicky and told us that he didn't trust this man. He thought he was dangerous. We knew this friend wouldn't harm any living thing, he was gentle, loving and respectful. This was either Journey's fear resurfacing or manipulation to get his own way.

The friend we had arranged to stay at our house called us from his sister's home across town. He agreed to stay there until the following day when we could re-address this situation with Journey.

Rex and I agreed that tough love was in order. We called Journey and, miraculously, he picked up his phone. "Journey, you are in our home. Move over. Adam is staying there, too. If you don't like it, find somewhere else to be for the next nine days."

The following day we couldn't reach Journey. He didn't answer his phone. No matter how many times I had to surrender Journey to his own devices, or how many times I placed him and all his affairs into the hands of God, it never got easier. I hated not knowing where he was. Not knowing if he were dead or alive.

Later that night we got an answer. A friend called,

"Uh, listen Rex, Journey showed up here last night on his bike. I am pretty sure he was intoxicated... He said some things that indicated he was a danger to others. I just wanted to let you know that after he left, we called the police. We gave them your address."

The following morning, the police showed up at our home and took Journey to CMH.

~

A week later we received a phone call from the case worker at the Grand Rapids hospital. She was just giving us a friendly update to let us know that Journey would be discharged on Monday. "I understand from Journey that he will be coming home to your house. Is that true?"

Well now, there was the question of the year. I told her that we hadn't heard from Journey at all. If he were to come home there would be requirements of him. He would have to stick to a treatment plan, either allopathic or naturopathic. It didn't matter to us, he could choose, but he would have to stick to one or the other. He would be required to have weekly family meetings to touch base, he would have to respect Rex and I, our property, and he would have to use the door instead of the windows. "Well, that all sounds reasonable to me. I will pass these things along to Journey..." I cut her off. "No, Journey needs to call us. He needs to hear these requirements *from us.* He will have to agree to these terms before he can come home. Please relay that."

That weekend we had class with Dennis and the rest of the Midwest fellowship. Dennis pulled us aside, "What are you thinking? Are you really considering letting Journey come back to your house? What makes you think that this time would be any different than the numerous other times?" Dennis was a little steamed but did his best to speak calmly. "If you let him come back, you will be adding to his problems, not helping him." And directly to me, "You have to stop enabling him. He has to learn from his mistakes." He maintained that Journey was a conscious being, doing his master's program. Not in a university, but in life. "If you treat him like a man, maybe he will start acting like one."

We asked ourselves what was different this time. The answer was nothing. We had extracted promises from Journey before. Many times. Journey seemed to resent us when he was home. He appeared to have little to no self-respect. He had turned 25 years old that spring. Perhaps it *was* time for him to take responsibility for himself.

In fact, I had just learned a working definition of "enabling" and it taunted me. Enabling someone was to do for them what they could do for themselves. I realized that I was doing it to avoid my own pain. My fear. My guilt. My sorrow. We had been enabling him, but of course I believed that we were helping him. But here's the rub, once you know something, it becomes impossible to unknow it.

Early Monday morning, we called the hospital and told them there had been a change of plans. "Do not bring Journey to our home. We will be coming down to see Journey in person. We will be there soon."

During the hour-long drive, I felt strangely calm. Peaceful, even. Tough love can be difficult, especially if a child is vulnerable somehow. But vulnerable or not, this decision felt like the right action.

Journey looked good. He seemed happy to see us. He explained that he had just been playing basketball and apologized for the sweaty hugs. We explained to Journey that we thought it was better for him, and for us, if he were to live outside of our home. There was a moment of surprise, a glistening in his eyes, but he handled it like a man. I told him for the umpteenth time that I trusted him to land on his feet.

He seemed both fragile and strong. Afraid and relieved. Maybe it was empowering for him to know that we believed in his ability to live on his own. Maybe he drew strength from our faith in him? Maybe.

Chapter 43

Journey was discharged from the hospital to Bridges in Lansing. From there, he and his caseworker began the search for safe and affordable housing. They applied for the first choice which was in East Lansing but learned that there was a four to six-month wait.

Journey asked if he could come home until that apartment became available. I wrote him a well thought out letter explaining why we thought it best if he continued to look for independent housing.

Journey asked a few family members if he could stay with them. No one felt like they could manage the stress of having Journey and his potential actions in their homes. One set of grandparents are in their eighties and live in Texas. My mom, his maternal grandmother, lives locally but her worrying makes mine look nonexistent. It wouldn't be a good fit for any of them. It was sad, and Rex and I wavered, but in the end, we were shored up by our belief that we were empowering Journey rather than enabling him.

We spoke with him frequently and helped with the search for a place to stay. Eventually, we found a place in East Lansing that, for a small fortune, would lease a small studio apartment month to month.

On October 1, 2012, Journey moved into his new digs. My mom, Breaha and I all pitched in to furnish the small space. Journey was appreciative of our efforts and seemed proud to have his own space. He and I saw each other every few days. Often after work I would stop by and pick him up to go for a bite to eat or walk across the street from his apartment to the little bar and play pool. Sometimes we would just drive around talking.

During one of those conversations, he shared with an authenticity I hadn't seen in a while and it brought me to tears. "I have so many regrets. There are a hundred things I wish I could redo. I have no friends left…" He quickly wiped at a tear. "I don't think it's possible to rekindle those old friendships either. Who would befriend someone who has so little to offer? I am 25 years old and I don't even have a job. I am on welfare for fuck sake!" Something about that statement made him laugh. We laughed together all the while our tears stained our faces. In his eyes, Journey had failed at the most basic of things: growing into manhood.

I never had a fair crack. All I wanted was to be manly and that was definitely the thing I was not.

~ *Journey, Summer, 2010*

The following week, we spent a whole afternoon going from place to place, picking up applications for employment. A few days later, we took some of them back and he confided that being productive would do wonders. "God, I would love to have a place to go every day. I need to be productive. I have a lot to offer and would like the opportunity to make a difference, no matter how small." I thought of how this is the most basic of needs: to be needed.

~

Sometime toward the end of October, Journey decided to go to Midland and spend a few days with Breaha and Zach. He was in good spirits when I picked him up that evening. I watched as he tossed a few personal items into his backpack. "Okay, I think that should do it." I saw his bottle of medication on the counter and said, "Oh, here. Remember your meds." Absentmindedly, he tossed them into his bag. "Oh yeah, thanks."

Walking toward the car, Journey raised his eyebrows a notch and motioned driving. He looked so happy and lighthearted. I knew how much he loved driving and he had always been a cautious driver. I tossed him the keys, "Sure, drive Miss Daisy!"

It was a glorious night. It was warm enough to have the moonroof open and there was a big, yellow harvest moon on the horizon. Journey took a deep breath, "God, it feels good to be alive! To feel the wind against my face, to have hope again!"

I remembered the bottle of medication that almost got left behind. I felt a tightening in my gut. I worried that he would be irresponsible and quit taking it cold turkey and without support and end up back where he had been countless times before. I took a breath and tried to make the next words sound casual. I wanted to say what was on my mind without alienating him. "Listen, Journ, about…" He sensed what I was about to say and cut me off two words in. "Mom, let's not spoil this moment. Please?" He smiled that brilliant smile and changed the subject.

Chapter 44

The following week I took Journey to Meijer to get a few groceries. Since I had a few items to purchase myself, I suggested we go our own ways to get the things we needed and meet back in 20 minutes.

When we met back up at the designated spot, Journey's cart was empty. His hands hung limply at his sides. He looked utterly dejected standing there. I fought to be calm, to make my voice sound nonchalant when I asked him why his cart was empty. My chipper façade didn't fool him. It never did. His face hardened, and he said he wasn't in the mood to deal with all the people. I asked him if he wanted to wait in the car and I would get his food, but he refused.

A few days passed, and I hadn't heard from Journey, so I texted him to see if he wanted to get some dinner after work. He replied via text, "No thanks. I just need some time to myself." From that point on, any invitation to see him was declined and he only responded occasionally to my texts. For days following that shopping trip, I wasn't myself. The memory of Journey standing there with the empty shopping cart haunted me. Many nights, sleep escaping me, I would wander aimlessly through the quiet house, stopping periodically to stare out a window into the dark and empty night. I was looking for something I couldn't name. Perhaps my soul knew that I had seen my son's face for the last time.

In November I asked Journey if he had any Christmas wishes. He texted back, "Yes, please. I would like a Carhartt coat. Tan. Size medium. Thank you."

The days turned to weeks and still none of us had seen Journey. A few times he asked me to bring him some groceries, but he was never there when I brought them by. He had "just left" or I would receive a text saying, "Please leave them by the door if you don't mind, it's taking me longer than I thought to get home."

One time he met me at the door and opened it just enough to take the bag I had brought. He blocked the door. Clearly, I wasn't invited in. He had a smile on his face, but it looked more like a grimace. He was trying to assure me that he was okay, but I am very familiar with his smile and the light it generates. This was not one of those smiles. It was harder to see him trying so hard to appear okay than it was to not see him at all.

On December 22, 2012, I felt buoyant at our winter solstice gathering. I informed my friends that a miracle had occurred, and I was planning to spend the whole month of February in retreat. My intuition had been nudging me for the past year to spend some time alone. It had been impossible to take any amount of time away from my job at the birth center and my private doula practice.

But then, remarkably, my schedule cleared. My whole life changed, actually. After a decade of serving families of Mid-Michigan, the birth center was forced to close. This left birthing families with fewer options and it left a handful of women, including me, jobless for the time being.

I had done my best to be a calm and loving force during that stormy time at the birth center. I had spent countless nights and days with my dying sister and was often stressed by my experience of witnessing Journey's chronic mental anguish.

Now, with no daily "job" to go to, my sister no longer sick, and Journey in his own apartment in East Lansing, I suddenly had a lot less responsibility. When I looked ahead at my birth schedule, I realized that I had no clients due at all in the month of February! Hallelujah! It had been years since I had five whole weeks in a row with no mamas due. It occurred to me that perhaps I could take that alone time that I had been fantasizing about.

~

Years ago, I had experienced a profound silent retreat weekend at a center called the Self Realization Meditation Healing Center (SRMHC). The SRMHC is one of five such centers worldwide, and it just so happens that the one in the United States is not only in the state of Michigan, it is twenty minutes north of Lansing in the city of Bath. I called the Center's live-in director and asked about availability in February. She was enthusiastic about having me come out and we decided that I would arrive on February first and stay until the end of the month. Whatever it was that spirit had in mind for me to do, I would have a lot of quiet contemplation ahead of me. I was ecstatic!

Chapter 45

There had been several times over the past couple of years when I was forced out of Journey's life both emotionally and physically. My heart ached with not seeing him or knowing if he was dead or alive. Sometimes during those absences, I would sit quietly and still my mind. I would call upon Journey. I would ask his soul to communicate with me. Not the mixed-up personality, but the true essence of Journey. Often, I would sense him, peaceful and wise. Sometimes in my mind's eye, I would see his face; usually just his eyes bright with light and love. I would breathe a bit easier and remind myself that he was okay. It wasn't the same as being with him or hearing his voice, but it was something.

Christmas was fast approaching, and we still had hope that Journey would stop the nonsense and come home for the holiday. Each of us called and texted but got no response.

Christmas morning, Rex awoke with a start. Immediately he was up and getting dressed. This was so unlike Rex on any morning, but especially so on Christmas morning.

"Rex, what's wrong? What are you doing?"

"I'm going to check on Journey."

"What? Right now? Wait a sec, I'll come with you." Rex made some lame excuse about not wanting to have to wait for me to get dressed, "Maybe you and Breaha could get started on those yummy Christmas muffins?" I appreciated his attempt at being upbeat, but I knew him better than that. He was worried and Rex, by nature, was not a worrier.

Zach, bless his heart, pulled on his jeans and boots and walked out the door with Rex. Within minutes they were out of the driveway and driving too fast through the sleepy subdivision.

Breaha and I pretended to discuss the brunch menu. We took things out of the refrigerator. Put them back in. We huddled on the couch warming our hands on our coffee mugs, comfortable enough in each other's company to sit in silence. We prayed for Journey and for Rex and Zach. We prayed for every family that would be celebrating the holidays without their loved ones.

A short time later Rex's car pulled into the driveway. I had already imagined the worst possible scenario; Zach would be driving, Rex sobbing, unable to look me in the eyes. He would try to be strong as he told Breaha and me that something dreadful had happened.

And because I was ever hopeful, I had also imagined the best scenario. Rex and Zach and Journey would get out of the car laughing; stomping the snow off their boots at the door, wondering what was for breakfast. But in real time, Rex was driving. He was not sobbing, and Journey was not with them.

When Journey moved into this apartment he had given us a key so that if he lost his, we would have an extra. Rex had taken the key that morning. When there was no answer to his knocks, he unlocked the door and found that Journey was not home. I don't know what Rex had dreamed or what he thought he might see, but finding Journey gone from his apartment was apparently a relief. Rex wasn't the anxious person that had left the house an hour earlier.

I was wondering where Journey was that early on Christmas morning. Denny's maybe? What else was open? We tried several times throughout the day to call and text but we got no answer. Josh came over later in the afternoon and we poked around at our dinner and half-heartedly opened gifts. No one was in the mood for games or pretenses.

I remembered Journey's boyish enthusiasm about Christmas and wondered what he was doing and why he wasn't home with his family. About 9 PM I couldn't stand being idle any longer; I got in my car and drove to East Lansing. I had to try something.

Journey answered my knock through the closed door. "Hey Journ, we've missed you today. There is still plenty of food, why don't you come home for a while?" He replied, "I am home. I am working. I won't be coming with you."

I tried again, "There are gifts for you...I think Santa brought you a new coat."

"Did you bring the coat?"

"No, Journey, I was hoping that you would come home and partake in Christmas..." There was a long silence. "Journey?" Still nothing. Was he reconsidering? Crying? Finally, I said "I am going to wait in my car for five minutes. If you change your mind, come on out. Even if it's only for an hour, one of us will bring you home. Okay?"

I waited fifteen minutes before I drove home alone.

Chapter 46

Rex thought that we should simply drop the coat off at his apartment and take all the other gifts back. "He is so inconsiderate. Why would we reward that behavior?" I was torn. It was inconsiderate, but he wasn't well, or he would have come home. Besides, I knew that he would love the cotton-cashmere hoodie. We are all fiber snobs when it came to clothes, the softer the better. I was excited to find something so luxurious and affordable but also masculine. And it could be machine washed. And warm socks? Well, it was a cold winter and Journey walked a lot. He only owned one pair of jeans. And then the set of warm flannel sheets were on sale, it would be hardly worth the effort to return them.

I gave Rex the receipts and told him that if he wanted to return all the gifts he could. Three days later the unopened gifts were still under the tree, a fine layer of dust collecting on the brightly colored paper. That morning, when I sat down to meditate, I couldn't settle. I don't know how long I sat there chasing down my errant thoughts, but eventually I gave up.

It was 19 degrees outside and Journey needed a coat. After getting dressed, I got onto my hands and knees and knelt for a moment by the tree. Right at eye level was one of Journey's favorite ornaments from childhood. I swallowed a lump that had formed in my throat and forced my eyes to focus on the packages. I was looking for the bigger one that contained the warm coat. Finding it, I swiped at the dust and shook off the brown needles that covered it. Tucking it under my arm like it contained life itself, I ran for the car.

Two doors west of Journey's apartment complex I saw a parked ambulance. And a police car. I continued to Journey's apartment, going through the motions, but I knew that Journey was in that ambulance. I knocked on his door and waited. There was no answer. I got into my car and drove two driveways over and pulled into the parking lot of the bicycle store. I pulled up next to the ambulance, "I think my son is in your ambulance," I said flatly. The EMT looked at the driver's license in his hand and said, "Is your son named…Journey?"

He opened the door and I saw the back of Journey's head nodding his assent to something the other attendant had asked him. "Hey Journey, your mom is here." With barely a glance in my direction, Journey waved me away. The gesture implied, "Go home, Mom."

"Your son called us a little while ago. He asked us to take him to the hospital to get some medication. Apparently, he burned his hair with a lighter too..." his voice trailed off. He wore a professional look, showing concern even though he had to be impervious to such things. "Has this ever happened before? Has your son had any recent episodes of.... depression? Or.... mental illness?" And then, as an afterthought, "I didn't realize that he'd called you too."

I felt numb, and my voice sounded like it belonged to someone else. "He has had some trouble before. And he didn't call me. I just came." I thought I was coming to bring him his coat, but the ambulance was toasty warm. The hospital would be warm, too. He didn't need the coat.

"Okay, well it's good that he called. He knew that he needed help. Your son will be in good hands." The EMT disappeared through the back of the ambulance. The brightly painted doors slammed shut. Blinking back my tears, I watched as they drove away.

It was true, he had called for help himself. That was a good sign. And he had asked to be picked up two doors from his apartment. Perhaps so his neighbors wouldn't see. That required forethought, too.

I used my key to let the officers inside Journey's apartment. They needed to make sure there was no meth brewing there, I guess. Satisfied that this crazy person wasn't a danger to his neighbors, they left me standing there surveying the mess.

I picked up a few things, gathered the dirty socks and discarded clothes into a bag. I didn't stay long, it was freezing in there. Turning to the thermostat, I noticed that Journey had thought to turn it down to 50 degrees. His electric heat bills were astronomical. The window was opened just a crack to air out the smell of singed hair. Numbly, I drove home, the wrapped package still on the seat next to me.

~

I learned from CMH that Journey was back in the Grand Rapids facility. The ninth hospitalization in three and a half years and only the second one that was voluntary. After a week had passed, I decided to take him a few belongings. I removed the holiday wrap from the hoodie, the new jeans and warm socks and a hat. I put them into a grocery bag and drove west. It wasn't visiting day, but I didn't care. I didn't think he would see me, but I wanted him to know that he was loved and cared for. I thought of the patches of hair that had been burned off with the lighter and figured he would appreciate the hat.

Chapter 47

On January 26, 2013, a Saturday morning, Rex got a call from Journey. "Hey Dad, would you mind picking me up at Bridges and taking me to the mall? Maybe we could hang out together afterward?" The times that Journey reached out and wanted to spend time with us were few and far between. Rex changed his plans and spent the whole day with him.

That night, Rex looked tired but content. It was a frigid evening and the steam coming off the jacuzzi made his face look otherworldly as he spoke. "I had an epiphany today. For the first time since Journey became symptomatic, I saw him as perfect. I felt calm and loving toward him. For once, I didn't want to 'fix' him. I just loved him exactly the way he was." He smiled, "We had a good time together, mostly shopping for the perfect nose ring, but we laughed and were authentic with each other. He thanked us for the Christmas presents. He really appreciates the warm coat." Tears streamed down his cheeks as he told me that he saw Journey as whole and perfect, maybe for the first time ever. "I have regrets about being so hard on Journey, but I am grateful for the new insights. Shit. It has taken me long enough, but do you know something? From here moving forward, I am committed to be the best person I can be. Journey really is a profound teacher." Toweling off and more lighthearted, he said, "I'm going to see him again on Wednesday. I'm taking him for a haircut and then to update his driver's license."

~

The following morning, Rex opted to go to church without me. I had decided to stay home and rewrite a guided meditation that I was planning to record the next day. Sipping my coffee, still in my jammies, I sat down at my computer to write.

An hour or so later I got up to stretch and looked out the window. There was a cop cruiser in my driveway. Police officers accompanied by a priest is never a good sign.

There's a reason people ask you to sit down before telling you devastating news. I wish that the officer had.

As soon as I heard, "I am sorry. Your son died this morning…" my knees buckled, and I fell to the floor. Staring at her black utilitarian-looking boots, I thought she must be wrong. Certainly, I would know, *would feel* if my son had left the planet? I struggled to get to my feet. The priest's hand appeared to help me up, but I crawled to the couch instead. I told the officer that she must be mistaken. "My name is Jeri. My son's name is Journey, but he is fine. My husband spent the day with him yesterday...I...I would know if he had died. I would *know*!" She shook her head. I looked imploringly at the other female officer. She looked down at her hands and said nothing.

I turned to the priest. "I know healers. We can pray over him. Is he (his body... I couldn't bear to think of Journey as a body) safe? Keep him safe until..." The priest shook his head. "No, I saw him Mitzi. I prayed for him. He is gone. He won't be healed..."

"What kind of priest are you? Do you work for God or not?" I hit him in the arm. Hard. "Jesus healed Lazarus! Please...hold the space for a miracle for my son!" I began sobbing uncontrollably. I curled up into a tight ball and covered my ears with my hands.

The priest didn't seem fazed by my assault on his arm or his character. He simply offered to pray with me. He prayed but my mind seemed to be moving in slow motion. It did occur to me to call Dennis; he is a healer after all.

He answered on the first ring. Of course, it was only 7:00 AM in California. I shouted at Dennis,

"Journey is dead! You're a healer, heal him! Bring him back!"

"What…? Mitzi what are you saying?"

"You heard me! Journey. He died. Apparently, he jumped off a building. If you are who you say you are, then heal my son!" I hung up.

Much to their credit, neither of the officers or the priest looked surprised by my outrageous statement. They simply asked me if I wanted to put some clothes on before we went to the church to tell Rex. I looked down at my tatty nightgown but still I couldn't pull it together. There was a strange ringing in my ears and I kept batting at them to get it to stop. Eventually, I made my way down the hallway to my bedroom, holding onto the walls for support, like someone twice my age. I went into my room and pulled things out of my closet. Numbly, I pulled on some clothes. I guess I looked presentable, because the priest nodded at me and said that I was doing well.

"Is there anyone else you need to call before we leave?" the officer asked. Breaha came to mind. She and I were planning to meet up later that day for some shopping. I began sobbing again. I glanced at the clock and knew that she was in the middle of teaching her Zumba class. My mind clicked into gear for a moment to register that Zach was at work. I called Breaha's mother-in-law. I don't recall what I conveyed, but I wanted her to get ahold of Zach and have him pick up Breaha. However, she went directly to the academy herself and told Breaha that I needed to talk to her right away. All I knew was that Breaha and Zach needed to come home as soon as possible and that I could not tell her this news over the phone. It was hours before she stumbled in the front door demanding to know what had happened. It must have been awful for her, wondering what had happened, who had died. Still, I don't know how it could have been done differently.

The first police officer began firing off questions, "Did Journey live here, with you? If so, can I look in his room? Do you think he left a note?" My mind was reeling, still trying to grasp what was happening. I stared blankly at her, but eventually told her that he had his own apartment in East Lansing. "Do you have a key?" The priest gave her a look and she stopped talking.

Carefully, he guided me out of the house and into the back seat of the police car. I thought of Rex and his innocence. He was sitting in the comfy chairs at church, filling his cup with spiritual nourishment. He had no idea that his life was about to come crashing down upon him. My heart ached, and I cried harder thinking about telling Rex that Journey had died.

Until that day, I had never been in the backseat of a police car. To my surprise, there were no cushions back there. The seats are made of hard fiberglass or some such thing that can't be destroyed, I guess. No comfort measures for criminals being hauled off to jail. No comfort measures for mothers carrying their broken hearts in their laps.

All the way to the church the priest and I prayed the Hail Mary. I wasn't raised Catholic, but I have a fondness for the Divine Mother. How could I not? Her presence is palpable at every birth.

For those of you that don't know, the last line of that supplication is "pray for us sinners now and at the hour of our death. Amen." Several years ago, I changed that last line to be more resonant with me and more appropriate for births. Not that I spoke it out loud, but sometimes I would find myself humming it or repeating it over and over like a silent mantra.

I had to change the last line, because who wants to consider death at an event as glorious as birth? So, I sought out a Catholic priest and asked him if he thought God or Mary would mind if I said the last part of that prayer my own way. After hearing my rendition, he smiled and patted my hand fondly and said he was sure that God would be fine with my version. So, my ending is simply "Pray for us now." The thing is, when I am saying it out loud with someone else, it throws everything off. The cadence is ruined. At the end of every round it's like a scratch in a record, an awkward moment. Then it occurred to me that this *was* the hour of my son's death. Perhaps the original version was more appropriate after all.

So, I put Journey's name in the place of "sinner" and the prayer rolled off our tongues, cadence intact.

Arriving at the church, I numbly took a seat in the vestibule. The officer headed right for the closed doors to the centrum. "What is she thinking?" my mind screamed. I stepped in front of the door and blocked her from opening it. Unbelievable. She intended to interrupt the last ten minutes of the service to give Rex this news?

My husband's life was about to change, his heart about to be broken open. This was going to be hard enough without having a uniformed police officer pull him from the service. We would allow him these last few minutes of peace.

For a glorious moment, I was livid. It was a welcome relief from the desperation. I wanted to slap her. Instead I simply said, "We will wait. Sit down and wait." After a few awkward moments, I tried for conversation. "Do you have children?" I asked her. "No, I don't," she smiled feebly. No surprise there.

The service ended, and people began pouring out of the centrum. Rex saw us all sitting there, and his face fell. To his credit, his body didn't. I wanted to encourage him to sit first, but the officer was pulling him into an open doorway. She told him before I could even make it to him. He simply cried, "Oh, no. No. No."

Chapter 48

Silently we drove to the hospital to see Journey. The walk through the parking structure and then the lobby was a blur. We ended up in a small window-less room. A staff person came in and told us that the medical examiner wasn't there on Sundays and we would have to wait until the following day to see Journey. Rex clearly and firmly told her to get someone from management. We weren't leaving until we saw him.

I don't know how long we waited. Minutes? An hour? A lifetime, really. It didn't seem right that an impersonal law put in place to assure a proper autopsy trumped the parents' need to see their son's recently vacated body. I added it to the ongoing mental list I kept, a list of things that I planned to advocate to change in my old age.

A few minutes into our wait, alarms began blaring

throughout the hospital. Sirens, muted through the thick walls of the hospital, sounded like they were coming from every direction. A woman rushed in to tell us that arrangements were made for us to see Journey, but before they could come and tell us, an emergency had taken precedence.

Breathlessly, she informed us, "A water main has just burst. Water is everywhere, flooding the hospital's east end. The morgue is under six inches of water." Shaking her head and making clicking sounds, she ushered us out of the room. The blaring sirens and alarms assaulted our senses. She promised to call as soon as it was possible to see him. "I get it," she assured us. "Someone will call you by the end of the day, definitely before the autopsy is performed."

Outside the hospital, fire trucks and police cars surrounded the place, parked at odd angles in a jumbled mess. I guess they were doing their job though, which was to keep all moving traffic away from the hospital. Vaguely I wondered why, when a building was flooding they would need a half dozen fire trucks, but just as quickly the thought vanished.

The wind was blowing in angry gusts and made strange, otherworldly whining sounds as it blew through the hospital's parking structure. For a moment if felt like the wind tore right through my body. I was a porous mass of electrons and protons whirling around a loose form that vaguely resembled my body. I felt like a sponge of flimsy nothingness held together only by a tiny gold disc in my heart area. Rex touched my elbow to guide me to the car, and my body went slamming back together, heavy and dense like it was numbed with Novocain. I shuffled to the car, my inner voice literally telling me to move one foot and then the other. I hauled myself into the car willing myself to simply breathe. It felt like there was something heavy sitting on my lap. I opened my eyes and looked but saw nothing there. I felt its weight, though. Grief and sorrow sat like unwelcome guests in my lap.

We arrived home and pulled into the driveway just as Breaha and Zach pulled up. Breaha stumbled up the walk looking stricken. Seeing both Rex and I she must have known that it was Journey.

I guess I hadn't learned a thing from my earlier experience. We should have waited until Breaha was sitting down, but as soon as she saw us she demanded to know what had happened. Her eyes were red from crying and red splotches dotted her pale cheeks. Barely inside the door, she insisted again. "Dad, what happened? Tell me what happened!" Rex, choking on his own tears said, "I am so sorry, honey. It's Journey. He died this morning." Even though Rex had a protective arm around her, she collapsed to the floor in pretty much the same spot I had earlier that morning. Zach and Rex gathered her up from the floor and guided her to the sofa. She slid from the couch back to the floor and sat there sobbing like a young child.

Almost 26 years ago in that very room Rex,

Breaha and I wept with joy at Journey's arrival. Now, here we sat in shock and disbelief at his departure.

~

Rex called Josh and learned that he was out with a friend. Rex asked him to come right away. And then to Josh's apparent inquiry, "No son, just you. And please, come as soon as you can."

A short time later Josh was standing just inside the door shaking his head and crying, "Oh, no. Not this. No." Rex gathered him into his arms. And so, we began the next chapter of our lives.

~

The evening of Journey's death, wracked with sorrow and disbelief, I stepped outside into the cool night air. I tried to still my mind to find Journey. How can a person be here one moment and simply be gone the next? There was no stillness to be found. I resorted to loud sobbing instead. "Journey, where are you? Oh God, what happened? Please. Please, don't be gone."

And then as plain as the nose on my face, I heard Journey's voice inside my head, "Everything is going to be okay, Mom. We've done the hardest part already." I thought that I must be hallucinating. How could we have done the hardest part already?

"How can *that* be? *You died* this morning!" There

was no response. The frigid January evening was dark and silent. `

A few days later, still incredulous that I didn't feel Journey leave this earth plane, I thought back to what I had been doing at the time of his death. I was writing. I was rewriting a guided imagery exercise to be in the first-person narrative. Here is exactly what I was writing when my son's soul slipped from his body:

> *"This is a time of gathering in...a time to nourish myself from my own Source of well-being...A time of letting go of disappointments and plans that didn't materialize. I release those that I have loved and nurtured that may now need their own freedom to fly in whatever way is best for them. I surround them with light and love.*
>
> *I release any unrealistic need to hold on...or control...or protect them. The same Source of love and light that is me...is also them. It guides and protects them just as it guides and protects me. I am letting go of the fear of endings and the fear of new beginnings. I now release any need for unrealistic guilt...unrealistic regret. In its place...faith, clarity and peace flow freely."*

Chapter 49

It's not that I set out to be contrary; it is just that often things that seem right and normal to me are in opposition with the world's view of right and normal. That whole "march to the beat of your own drum" resonates perfectly with me.

When we learned that Journey died, we didn't automatically assume that we would have a memorial. However, after the excruciating job of informing loved ones of the news and then watching as Breaha wrote her own brother's obituary, the next thing was to decide if we would indeed have a memorial.

Josh, Breaha, Zach, Rex and I sat together poking around some delicious smelling food that had mysteriously arrived for dinner. "I don't want to do a memorial just for the sake of doing it," I stated. "Why would we have one? What would we want to achieve?" After a brief conversation, I answered my own question. For me, there were two reasons to put ourselves through such a painful ritual. First and foremost, I wanted Journey's soul to experience the huge love that was surrounding us. I wanted the profound love of our community to envelop him like it was enveloping us. I hoped that all that love would be his companion, accompanying him to the next place.

Secondly, I knew that because of the nature of Journey's illness, his relationships had suffered. There were a lot of people that carried guilt and regret and it was only amplified by learning that he had died. I knew vaguely then what I know now with certainty; if their pain surfaced in the presence of love, it could begin to heal.

We chose Saturday, February second as the best possible day for the memorial. I chose noon since that is the time that Journey was born, and it was the only time that came to mind.

We learned later from a numerologist that the date Feb 2, 2013 was a number 10. Ten is the number for completion. It occurred to me that that Journey's apartment number in East Lansing was also #10, and the room at Bridges, the step-down facility where he was staying when he died, was #10.

A few months prior, between my prayers, researching and worrying, I invested in an Eastern astrology reading for Journey. The takeaway for me was that this well-known astrologer from India whose name I could not pronounce, told me that Journey's chart did not indicate the chart of someone who was here for creation. This was the chart of someone who was here for completion. He also said that come early 2013 "there was likely to be an abrupt shift in the order of things." My naïve heart skipped a beat. I remember hoping that perhaps springtime would bring healing for Journey.

~

The morning of the memorial arrived bringing heavy snow. The cold, muted weather matched my feelings that day. It felt oddly like I was moving through someone else's life. That morning I prayed that I could stand upright. In other words, not pass out or fall apart. And that I could keep my heart open; keep love present even in my sorrow.

The church where we held the memorial seated 400 people and from where I sat, it appeared that most of the seats were occupied. We heard stories of Journey's childhood, high school and college days from the perspective of others that knew and loved our boy. And, an amazing thing happened. The people who came in to the church distraught, tearful and full of regret approached us afterward with gratitude and lighter hearts. One woman asked me, "What just happened? I could never imagine a memorial could be so sad and so loving at the same time." I only smiled in return. Honestly, I didn't know what had just happened.

My prayer had been answered. I did not fall on my face, nor did I fall apart emotionally. People seemed to benefit from the loving presence that was generated, and most importantly to me, I knew that Journey was bathed in love and shored up for the next leg of his, well, journey.

Let me make something clear, though. It is true that there were a lot of loving people at Journey's memorial. It is also true that I felt embraced by, even lifted by, that love. Still, it was the second worst day of my life. My heart ached with a longing that I knew would not be fulfilled. I was devastated to be saying goodbye to Journey.

Chapter 50

I think I drove myself to death out of greed for understanding the soul. I was given many bits of understanding, with an option to return to my ignorance, but I did not. I remember a bible story where a man was tempted to indulge in knowledge. That knowledge cast him from his ignorant bliss. I can relate.

~Journey, Spring, 2010

The evening of Journey's memorial, we had a conversation with Blair, a longtime friend that we knew through our spiritual studies with Dennis. As soon as I saw him, a memory flashed in my awareness. The memory of a conversation he and I had two summers prior. We were sitting in the warm sun on our deck, and he told me he thought he understood what Journey was experiencing. "After college, I spent several hours a day in meditation. Some days I would be 'gone' for five or six hours at a time. I reached a point during one of my meditations where I knew if I kept going, crossed the line so to speak, that I might not come back. At least, not all the way." He looked pointedly at me and continued, "I stopped meditating so much. I limited it to a couple of hours a day. I was so ungrounded, spacey and 'out of my body' so often that I had a hard time functioning in daily life. Finally, I admitted myself into the hospital. While there, I took medication for a while to slow down my racing mind and to help ground me. I think that something similar may have happened with Journey...only he didn't stop, he kept going."

Blair sought us out that evening after the memorial, to tell us something he felt certain about. It was his belief that Journey did not intentionally commit suicide. He explained, "The morning Journey died, I experienced a profound meditation. At the time, I did not know how Journey died, but I saw him step off a building believing he could fly."

The days and nights after the memorial blurred together and seemed to hold little or no meaning. We walked around aimlessly, slept and ate at random times and held each other closely. It was a time of stark contrast. Our home was filled with deep sorrow but also profound love and Grace.

I recalled the solstice gathering just a few weeks earlier, where I enthused about my upcoming retreat.

There was an intentional time set aside that evening where each person offered up a request for the new year, something that would support their spiritual growth or simply bring them more joy.

I asked to understand the practice of self-love. There was still a pattern within me that believed everyone else's needs were more important than my own. It had always been easier for me to extend love outward than to open my heart and receive it, so I asked God to reflect all the love that I had given to the community back to me.

Here I stood, five weeks later, with my community showering me with love. So much love in fact, that it felt like my feet did not touch the floor. I know that sounds like fantasy, but I felt as though there was a cushion of air between my feet and the ground. I had always heard the phrase "lifted up in prayer" but until then I had no idea that was a real thing. Cards and thoughtful letters arrived by the droves. Friends stopped by with pots of warm soup and hand-crafted art. There were prayer shawls and flowers, trees to plant and sometimes just a hug at the door. That week and for three months to follow, meals miraculously showed up at dinnertime.

Chapter 51

A few days after Journey's memorial a friend called to check on me. "You're still going to the retreat center?" She asked, incredulous. "I can't imagine being alone at a time like this."

"Yes, I am still going." I said with more certainty than I felt. "It has been planned for months. I think I am supposed to go." Clearly this wasn't going to be the retreat that I was excited about just a few short weeks ago, but the timing was impeccable, and I didn't know what else to do.

Rex was going ahead with previous plans to do business in Chicago. Lost in our own thoughts, we packed what we thought we would need for our individual trips. Rex was planning five days. I had four weeks if I wanted to be gone that long.

I arrived at the SRMHC in the evening with surprisingly few things. I carry my own pillow and bedding everywhere, even to the plushest hotels, so that was a given. In short order, I had my bed made, covered the small table in the room with a cloth and placed on it a photo of Journey and a candle. Journey's picture looked lonely and I made a mental note to put some flowers or a plant there as soon as I was able. I unpacked my journal and the one book that I brought with me.

I sat on the bed and looked around the room. "Here I am, God. Now what?" Silence. I had hours, days, the rest of my life ahead of me. I struggled to understand how I was going to make it through the night, let alone the rest of my life, without Journey.

There are no electronics at the center. The home is blissfully absent of televisions, radios, cell phone usage, microwaves and there is only minimal computer use in the office at specific times. It is designed that way to support those of us retreating to find the silence within.

I began a juice fast and spent the next 72 hours curled up on my bed. I got up for brief moments to use the restroom or get an occasional glass of juice or cup of tea. I wore an eye mask and earplugs although the ear plugs weren't needed. I thought that if I could close out all worldly stimuli then I might be able to see Journey again. I prayed for a lucid dream where I could hold him one more time, feel his breath against my cheek, ask him the questions that were raging in my heart. But, I had no such dreams.

Instead, I saw visions of my sons crumpled body lying on the concrete. I saw his body lying in the morgue with the resuscitation equipment still in his mouth, the blanket flat at the bottom where his broken feet lie under the sheet. I hated these thoughts and images, but I welcomed them anyway. I knew that they would haunt me my whole life if I didn't meet them head on and embrace them with love. I knew that I had to welcome my sorrow. I had to look at every image, however tragic, that my mind produced. I had to feel the anger, shock, and grief one by one as they surfaced. I knew that if I allowed these painful thoughts and feelings to surface in the presence of Love they could begin to heal.

I lost track of whether it was day or night. I slept periodically, prayed fervently, screamed into my pillow and breathed through my pain. At one point, I had a simple dream, an image of hundreds of people lifting me up in prayer. Whatever work I was doing, although I was alone, I was not alone.

It occurred to me that grieving is a lot like laboring, only in reverse. Instead of the waves of discomfort that bring our children into the world, there are waves upon waves of pain as we are forced to accept their departure. Just like labor, the pain comes in waves, followed by moments of respite, sometimes even profound insight. It is work that only the mother can do, although she will have loving support around her. Whether we are laboring to bring our children to this earth or letting them go, breathing is often the only way to successfully navigate from one wave to the next.

One night, sleep escaping me, I took a cup of tea and a couple of blankets out to the balcony swing. It was a crisp February evening. I had no idea what time it was, but the sky was dark as pitch, the new moon as invisible to me as my son. Intellectually, I knew that the grieving process required letting go. Letting go of hopes and dreams we have for our children. Letting go of their happy wedding day, or their delight as they became parents themselves.

My "letting go" was being held up by a fear that I might forget something. What if I forgot the shape of Journey's jawline? His hands? The sound of his laugh or the way his smile lit up the room? The thought of forgetting something, anything, had me paralyzed and holding on.

Again, I prayed for help. I felt a deep warmth rise within me. It was freezing out there on the balcony and the tea I cradled in my hands was barely luke-warm. This warmth was gentle as a breeze and it came with a tenderness that I have come to recognize as the Divine Mother. I felt wrapped in an immense hug, gentle and yet powerful. As soft as a whisper and as vast as the countryside around me. I knew that I was being held in the arms of Love. I also knew that I was one with that very same love. I was reminded of Journey telling me three Christmases ago that he had woken up feeling loved beyond measure and was equally aware that he was that same love.

Something profound happens when you are broken wide open and then touched by Grace. There are no words to describe it and any attempt would fall woefully short. I simply breathed a huge sigh of relief and uttered my profound gratitude. I sat silently as long as possible to bask in its wonder.

I then felt inclined to gather my precious memories of Journey. His smile, his humor, his sorrow, his brilliance, his love of others. On and on I went, sorting through my mind's most cherished memories. I knew then that this place that was being prepared in my heart was a conduit for love to flow from me to Journey and from him to me. It was a part of me and it could never be taken from me. I felt the grip around my heart loosen just a bit. I knew in that moment that our love, Journey's and mine, was eternal and it existed within me, as me. I slept like a baby that night.

Occasionally, I would size up a tree wondering if its branches reached six stories; some perverse part of me still needing to know how far Journey fell. My mind still offered up images of my son's broken body on the pavement, but I noticed with some amazement that these images came less frequently and when they did surface there was much less panic. I was a witness observing something tragic, but I was not seized by it. I decided that whenever my mind offered up an image that didn't serve me, I would hand it over to God. I simply took the fearful pictures and placed them on an imaginary altar in my mind. I would consciously imagine Journey in the arms of the Beloved, surrounded by light and love. It worked. Those images slowly began to subside.

After I had been at the Centre for about three weeks, I woke up one day and knew that it was time to go home. I made plans to leave the following morning. That afternoon in the porch swing, I began to contemplate my life at home. I began sobbing again. To no one and to everyone I cried, "What am I supposed to do now? I have no idea what is expected of me! So many chapters of my life have slammed closed… I am broken wide open and I am too tired to go looking for the next thing. Whatever you want me to do God, you had better put it right in my lap. And make it so clear that even with my bloodshot and swollen eyes I won't miss it."

The night that I returned home I was visited by a friend. She and Journey and I all share the same birthday, and from the day I met her, I felt a sisterly connection. When Journey was eight years old, he told me that, if he was an adult, he would marry her. She is one of those friends that I can see once a week or once a season and we just take up where we left off.

However, the night I returned from the center, she was anxious to see me. She wanted to come right then to tell me something important. "I have to see with my own eyes that you are doing okay…"

An hour later, she was sitting on my couch telling me about an evening of extraordinary dreams she had experienced a few weeks prior. She began, "A few weeks ago, I had the most bizarre night. I was awakened over and over by dreams of Journey and then of you. In the first dream, Journey showed up. He looked good." She gave me a sad smile. "Like himself, but he had an urgent message. He wanted me to contact you right away and tell you that you could not reach him. He wanted me to tell you that it wasn't possible without you dying. 'Tell her it's not her time.'" I sat stunned, thinking of my desperate attempts to reach him after arriving at the healing center. Of course, I had told no one. "Anyway" she went on, "I finally got back to sleep and right away had another dream. This time you were telling me that you had questions for Journey. You needed answers. You were adamant. You were crying and told me that you could not and would not accept that you had seen him for the last time." She looked at my face which must have shown my surprise. "I know. Weird, right? But there's more. The next dream, Journey was more insistent. 'Tell Mom to think about Breaha. And Dad and Grandma. She needs to stay for them. *She can't come here! It isn't her time.*'"

"This shit went on all night long," she laughed.

Feeling relieved to have translated the message to

me, grateful to no longer be responsible for getting those words from her head into mine, my friend gave me a fierce hug and got up to leave. At the door, she said "I am so glad to see that you are doing so well, Sis." I closed the door and stood against it taking in what she had just told me. I couldn't help but feel dejected. If Journey could show up so vividly and have present time conversations with her, then why not me?

Truth be told, I knew the answer before I even uttered the question. I was attached. I needed it, and desperation and neediness did not resonate with Journey's essence. Those qualities never resonated with him, even when he was in a body. He consistently railed against any pushiness or demands that I made, even when I coated them with niceties, explicit logic or reason.

I was reminded of that first week after Journey's death when I felt his presence near me. Most often, they were the times during the ebbs of the raging storm. The "in between times" when I was not thinking or demanding answers. During those times of complete and utter openness, when I had no agenda, only love, I felt Journey. I felt his love for me and his compassion. They were brief and fleeting moments of immense love; a lot like my experience of God's love, only these impressions were accompanied by Journey's unique essence.

~

Knowing that our love flowed easier when I wasn't demanding it, I became highly motivated to heal my pain so that I could experience that connection to Journey's love. I began to understand that the only time Truth really exists is in the present moment. The past is riddled with regret, the future is often accompanied with fear. The present moment can bring profound peace. It is where we have the true and meaningful moments in life.

Knowing something and living it are two different things, of course. Experiencing the present moment takes practice, and lots of it. As much as I strove to be present, experiencing my pain and breathing through it, I wasn't always able to do that. I seemed to spend as much time wondering, "What if?"

Chapter 52

One summer day when Journey was living with us and believed that he was dying of an unknown disease in his colon, he and I had a candid conversation. With utmost sincerity, I told him if I had to choose to never see him again, but I knew with certainty that he was safe, happy and healthy, I would choose that over knowing that he was suffering. His eyes met mine, deep pools of compassion and sadness. He gave me a weak smile and shook his head. "Nope, I don't think so, Mom."

My mind diligently went to work serving up images for me to examine, pictures of Journey, in another country, perhaps. He was healthy and living a joyful life, his smile brightening the space around him, just not around me. There was Journey, happy and full of life, but estranged from me, his mother.

Yes, that would be better than a life of suffering.

That was better than being a young man of 23 who ached with loneliness and had a brilliant mind that he couldn't trust. With new found resolve, I met Journey's eyes. I told him that my conviction was not dependent on his belief or disbelief. I said it and I meant it.

Three years later, Journey is somewhere else, and I will never see him again. He is safe and most certainly not suffering. And how am I doing? Am I fine with it? How did it escape me that death fit that description as well as anything else?

Chapter 53

In early March, five weeks after Journey's death, Dennis and his wife Jessica came to Michigan and spent a few days with us. I had a lot of questions for Dennis but couldn't formulate most of them at the time. I did, however, have two things that I knew we had to do and that I wanted his support with. One was opening the sealed box of Journey's ashes and the other was to go to the parking structure where he died.

The parking structure is in East Lansing. I knew I couldn't avoid it forever and yet I hadn't been able to drive anywhere near it, either.

On the drive to East Lansing, Rex seemed calmer than I knew he must have felt. In that first week after Journey died someone told me that experiencing a child's death would either end a marriage or create a stronger, more loving and compassionate relationship. I knew when I heard it that it had to be true. In that moment, with Rex driving us to the parking structure and many more after that, I knew that our marriage would be stronger. It was a weird dichotomy to feel such fierce love and appreciation and at the same time feel like grief and sorrow were threatening to choke the life out of me.

As soon as we came to the fork in the road in East Lansing, I had a visceral response to my emotional pain. I began shaking uncontrollably and felt like I couldn't breathe. I wanted to scream and climb out of my body but there was nowhere to go.

Rex drove in wide circles around the parking structure and then stopped the car a few blocks away so that we could see the parking deck in the distance. Rex and Dennis invited me to take as much time as I needed and to say and do whatever felt right. I felt angry and told them so. I yelled at the world. I felt the bitter sting of regret. I wiped snot on my mittens and didn't care. I yelled and hit the car seats. I sobbed in disbelief. I cancelled my goal to have saved Journey. Cancelling one's goals is one of the steps in the process of true forgiveness. The weight lifted just slightly. I could look at the parking deck for three full breaths before I had to look away.

I was as ready as I was ever going to be and told them so. Rex was able to find a parking place on the street, so we didn't have to park in the ramp. This was my first time being here, but Rex had come once right after Journey died. At that time, Rex had spoken with two local employees who witnessed Journey's fall and had stayed with him until the ambulance came. Journey had asked one of them to help him stand up. He also told them that his blood pressure was rising and asked if one of them could call an ambulance for help. During that time Rex had also spoken with one of the two police officers that had been at the scene. That officer told Rex that he thought Journey was trying to "stick the jump" which is a term used by college kids that do stupid things on a dare.

"Only from the bystanders and then, later, the footprints on the roof could I accept that your son fell from six stories." Shaking his head slightly, he gazed up at the structure, "You know, typically someone committing suicide doesn't land on their feet and then ask for help standing up."

Since Rex had been there the week after Journey died, he knew the exact spot where he'd landed. We walked up to the spot and numbly stared down at the concrete. It looked like any other patch of dirty city sidewalk. I imagined Journey lying there asking one of the bystanders to help him get up, his feet broken to bits inside his sneakers but still thinking he could stand. I thought of the countless times I had told Journey that I trusted him to land on his feet. A wave of nausea rose up and I choked on a sob. Dear God, that was only a figure of speech! But...what if Journey, in his confused state, took those words literally? He had stepped off a six-story building and landed on his feet. I wiped hastily at the tears that had begun to fall and tried to imagine what could have been going through his mind prior to taking that step. And then, I heard Journey's voice in my head as plain as day, *"You can't figure it out, Mom. Please, stop trying."*

Rex gently asked, "Honey, are you ready to go?" I nodded. I began walking toward the elevator and he and Dennis toward the car. We all realized at the same moment that we weren't on the same page. They looked at me with questioning eyes. "We aren't done yet. We have to go up. There." I gestured to the top of the building.

We rode the elevator up the six stories to the roof. Both Rex and Dennis walked immediately to the edge where Journey must have stepped off. They were patient while I walked around looking for answers that weren't there.

Eventually, I moved closer to the edge. There was a pile of dirty snow pushed up against the short wall that bordered the edge of the roof. I collapsed on to the snow bank and sobbed. I wailed into the wind wordless sounds that carried the grief of a thousand mothers. Mothers who had lost their sons at this very spot. Mothers who had lost their sons for as long as time existed. I felt vast and primal as my voice and the wind tore through my very soul.

And then, emptiness.

Two strong arms, one on either side of me,

brought me to my feet. I still hadn't gone all the way to the edge of the roof, but I felt like I had been to the edge of creation and back. I was suddenly cold and exhausted, "I am ready to go now."

Both Rex and Dennis just stood there, their love for me palpable. Neither of them moved away from the wall. "I'll come back another time and get close to the wall. I will look over the edge another time."

Rex said, "I knew that's what you were thinking. Are you sure you don't want to do it now while we are here with you?"

Shit. He was right. "Fine," I said mostly to myself as I took the three steps to the edge.

Standing there looking out over the rooftops, I told myself that after what I had been through, surely, I could look over the edge. This was just a formality. Without another thought, I looked down to the spot on the pavement where we had just been moments before. Instead of the familiar quiver that I usually feel looking down from high places, I felt energy moving up and down from me to the pavement. Surprisingly, there was no emotion. I didn't feel Journey or imagine his despair, I simply felt this tangible energy that seemed to be cleansing me and the area around me. After a few breaths, I stepped away. I felt lighter and freer. I knew that in the future I could drive through East Lansing, even walk by this parking garage and not fall apart.

On the way home, Dennis thanked me for my

courage. "You have no idea the amount of healing that has just taken place. Not only for yourself but for the community, the planet and all of creation." I didn't really understand how that could be, but in the core of my being I knew that he was right.

Chapter 54

The following day, feeling all shored up by my success at the parking garage, I suggested we open the box of ashes. I don't know why I couldn't bring myself to do it or ask Rex to do it without support. It seemed insurmountable.

My courage lasted as long as it took to get the box out and set it on the table. I got myself all worked up and told them to let me know when it was opened. For some reason, I thought that they would have to use power tools to open it. Have you ever seen one of those cremation boxes? They look as tight as a tomb.

I lay curled up in a tight ball in my bedroom bracing myself for the sound of the electric saw or the power drill. Jess came in and curled around me, holding me while I waited, my eyes squeezed shut and my hands over my ears.

About five seconds later Dennis said, "Okay, Mitz.

It's opened." Huh? So soon? I cautiously made my way from my bedroom back to the kitchen. The container was opened and next to it lay the butter knife that he had used to pop the lid off.

The box itself was smaller than a shoe box. I peered inside at the compact and yet heavy bag of gray ash, all that was left of a full grown physical body. By the grace of God, I was able to stand there knowing that this bag of carbon ash was not my son.

Dennis was going to take some of the ashes back with him to place on Mt. Shasta where he lives. As he was taking out a scoop of ashes I noticed something in the bag that was a different color and texture than the rest of the contents. I pointed to it and Dennis reached in and pulled out a large steel bolt. How does a bolt end up in a bag of human remains? We decided it must have worked loose from the furnace during the cremation process.

"What is *that* doing in there?" I demanded. The whole experience was becoming more and more surreal. Dennis grinned as he held it up for us to examine it. "What? Why are you smiling like that?"

"Well," he said, "the metal has held the electromagnetic charge of the carbon ash." Seeing the blank look on my face set him into teacher mode.

"When a person dies, and the soul leaves the body, that soul is responsible to impart all of its earthly experiences and knowledge back to the Wholeness. It does that by using electrical current for the mental body, color and liquid for the emotional body and carbon for the physical body." I sat down, still not comprehending what Dennis was saying. "The carbon remains of a cremated body holds an electromagnetic charge for a certain period of time. Each molecule is a hologram of everything that person knew, learned and experienced. When the carbon ashes are put on the earth, things with a similar charge are attracted to the molecules and they are then able to grow from that knowledge."

I imagined for a moment putting Journey's ashes on the ground in meaningful places. Maybe in this small way I could help him complete his work on the physical plane.

~

The following week on a cheerless March day, I got into my car with a small bag of Journey's ashes. I intended to take them to a few places where Journey had played as a child or loved as an adult. At each place, I offered a prayer. I thanked Journey for all the lessons he had taught me and was continuing to teach me, and then put a small amount of his carbon on the ground, in a stream or in the crook of a tree.

Eventually I found myself driving down a familiar country road in Williamston. It became clear that there was one more place I wanted to go before heading home for the day. I drove over a small bridge that spanned Deer Creek and pulled my car to the side of the road. The pale winter sun was descending quickly toward the western horizon and offered little in the way of warmth or comfort.

Deer Creek is a little stream where the kids had spent many happy hours splashing around with their friends. It seemed appropriate to put some of Journey's ashes there. A wave of sorrow and regret washed over me as I stood on the small bridge and tipped the bag toward the water. Out of nowhere a gust of wind swept in and dispersed the ashes into nothingness. Angrily, I kicked the railing in front of me and raised my fists to the sky. "I wanted those ashes in the stream!" Opening my hands, I noticed they were covered with a fine gray powder. Without a thought, I schlepped down to the water's edge and plunged them into the icy water.

Cold and exhausted, I got into my car. An unexpected peace washed over me. The interior of my car was filled with an exotic fragrance, unlike anything I had ever experienced. It was floral, sort of rose-like, but not in a fake, perfumey sort of way. I closed my eyes and inhaled deeply.

It was there for one breath, maybe two, and then gone. I felt uplifted. Invigorated. On impulse, I looked around my car for the source of the aroma. Intellectually, I knew of course, that I would not see my back seat filled with fresh flowers, but I couldn't keep from checking anyway. Seeing only shadows in the back seat, my mind immediately began to wonder if I had made it up. I leaned back in my seat, closed my eyes, and for the dozenth time, I asked, "Where are you, Journey?" And, like all the other times, I heard Journey's voice inside my head, *"I am everywhere."* Imagining Journey being "everywhere" wasn't a comfort to me. I thought of the vast universe and beyond and how very impersonal it seemed. Everywhere was akin to nowhere.

And then, there was an addendum, *"Mom. Everywhere **includes** here."* Oh, my God. He was right! *Everywhere* would indeed include *right here.* With me. In this car. In this moment. All the little hairs raised on my neck, down my back and on my arms. I felt a zing of energy move through my body. My heart felt lighter and much to my surprise, my lips lifted into an authentic smile.

Later that night, I was awakened from a dream. Since I rarely slept deeply enough to remember, or probably even have dreams, remembering any dream was significant. This one was extraordinary though, because it was of my beloved Journey. There were no words, just his presence and the profound love that we share. In the dream, he was standing in the doorway of my bedroom, casually leaning against the door jamb watching over me as I slept. I woke up to find my bedroom filled with that same exotic scent. Like before, it lasted just long enough to recognize its wonder, and then it was gone.

Chapter 55

That June, six months after Journey's death, Rex and I arrived home from a day of biking and swimming. Before we even made it into the house, our neighbor hailed us from over the fence. "Hey, you guys have a visitor! Look on the roof of your shed. It has been there all day." Confused but intrigued we went to the backyard to see what our neighbor was talking about. There on the roof of our shed was a large pigeon. This beautiful black and white bird acted perfectly at ease in our backyard. Seeing us, it flew off the roof of the shed and down into the yard about fifteen feet from us. Our neighbor laughed and said, "It's a messenger pigeon, maybe it has a message for you."

When I awoke the next morning, I looked out and saw the pigeon sitting on top of a statue in our backyard; the statue of an angel that we bought after Journey died. It perched there for a while before hopping around in the gazebo like it owned the place. I did a quick search for "messenger pigeons" on the computer and learned that messenger pigeons, also known as homing pigeons, sometimes lose their way. Or, they grow weary of flying across the continent and may decide to take a rest before moving on. The website said that offering water and perhaps some seeds would be helpful and that usually after a few hours the bird would take flight. My house is full of grains and seeds, so I made a feast of millet, quinoa and pepitas and put them on the grass just off the deck.

The pigeon enjoyed the breakfast I had prepared and even came up to eat while we were on the deck. It came so close that we were able to read the registration letters on the tag around its leg. We learned that it had flown all the way from California and was on its way home to Bath, Michigan which is just a few miles north of where we live. That was hard to fathom. How do you train a bird to do that? How can a bird weighing less than a pound fly well over a hundred miles in one day? I took lots of photographs as it strutted around our yard or made itself comfortable on the roof of the shed or gazebo.

The second day the pigeon was with us, I received a call from a school friend. "Hey, Mitz" she began, "My sister's friend's son would like to talk to you and Rex. His name is Nate and he works at the Marriot," she hesitated and went on, "the one across the street

from the parking garage…. where Journey died."
My heart did a little flip-flop in my chest. I learned
that Nate was one of the bystanders that stood with
Journey while they waited for the ambulance to
arrive. My friend went on, "It's been six months and
he hasn't forgotten Journey. He thought that the urge
to talk to you would go away, but it hasn't. Would you
and Rex be interested in talking with him?" I nodded
my head at the phone and then realized I hadn't
answered. "Yes, sure. That would be great. Thanks."
She gave us his name and phone number and told us
that he would be expecting our call. An hour later,
we spoke and set a date to meet the following day at a
restaurant in the mall.

Nate seemed very familiar to both Rex and me.
This meeting could have been extremely awkward,
but instead there was an effortless rapport between
us. He and Rex talked easily back and forth, making
small talk with lots of eye contact. And then without any fanfare, he put down his fork and looked
directly at me and then Rex. "I don't think that your
son committed suicide," he stated without preamble.
There was a pregnant pause while we waited for an
explanation. He took a deep breath and holding eye
contact went on, "I know that this sounds weird,
but sometimes I just know things. I don't know
how I know them, but I do." He explained that he
saw Journey come off the building feet first, not like
a person that had thrown themselves off a building

to die. "A few people had gathered, and one woman was praying quietly. Journey looked at me and we held each other's gaze for a long moment. He had the most peaceful look on his face, almost like a look of wonder. I just don't believe that he intended to die."

I recalled the look on my sister, Lana's face as she took her last breath. I hoped with all my heart that Journey had witnessed the same miraculous awe when he died.

I waited for Nate to say something more. Something definitive. But there were no facts, just a young man with clear eyes, a big heart and a willingness to be vulnerable.

As if reading my mind, our young friend went on to say that he had no concrete evidence to his theory. His voice trailed off. He repeated that he didn't know how he knew, but in his heart, he knew that Journey's death was an accident. We thanked him for taking the time to meet with us, for caring enough about Journey to ask us questions about his life. Essentially, this young man had shared with us his truth and that would have to be enough.

We finished our meals, said our goodbyes and drove home, our moods subdued. My spirits lifted a centimeter as I considered our backyard resident, the messenger pigeon. For whatever reason, I derived a ridiculous amount of pleasure watching it vacation in our yard.

I stepped out onto the deck looking in all the

pigeon's favorite places, but the bird was gone. My very conventional neighbor's words echoed in my mind, *Maybe the messenger pigeon has a message for you.* I wondered if God or Journey wanted me to know that he did not intentionally commit suicide. I had to admit that it was odd. This was the fifth person that told us they didn't believe Journey intended to die that day.

In the weeks following Journey's death, four unrelated people told me that they believed Journey's death was unintentional. These people came from all walks of life and three out of four of them had a similar idea about Journey's intentions on the day he died.

The first was a friend who studies physics. He told us that Journey was fascinated with and had been talking to him about levitation. The next, was our friend Blair, who spoke with us after the memorial. He had confided that he saw very clearly in a meditation, Journey standing at the edge of a building believing full well that he could fly. This was before he knew how Journey had died. Inwardly, I smiled sadly as Blair told me this. I was remembering six-year-old Journey jumping off the roof of my grandma's shed with an umbrella because he thought he could fly, and again a year later off our roof believing the same thing.

The third person was a devoted Christian woman who carries a Bible in her purse and prays faithfully for her loved ones and humanity. She stopped by to say that she had been praying fervently for Journey's soul, believing he had committed suicide, when God revealed to her that Journey was indeed with Him and that things aren't always as they seem.

The fourth person shared with us that she had a vivid dream. In it, Journey stepped off a building and floated gently to the ground.

I confess, as a mother considering her son's death, it felt better to think that somehow in his confusion, Journey thought he could levitate or fly off that building rather than intentionally stepping off to end his life. I asked myself if it really mattered. I know some would say it mattered greatly. An accident meant one would experience everlasting peace. Correspondingly, suicide would equate to a life of eternal suffering.

I am of the mindset that our Creator, the Omnipotent parent, is a loving Being. I could never accept the story that God is a vengeful father, one who would punish its beloved child, no matter what mistakes he or she has made, to a life of endless suffering. I am a regular ole *human* parent, and I would cut off my arm before I would condemn my child to hell. How could the almighty parent of all creation have less compassion than I? I abide by the belief that God and Love are synonymous, and that Journey resides in that love regardless of how he died.

Chapter 56

A few days after our pigeon took flight, Rex left for a business trip to Chicago. I stayed home because I had commitments to pregnant mothers and their soon-to-be-born babies.

I hadn't really thought much about the autopsy report, but one day during Rex's time away I couldn't stop thinking about it. I decided to follow my gut and read it. I put on someone else's face, and with someone else's eyes, read it with the same objectivity that I use when reading the news. Later, I wondered how I had summoned the courage to read that report, but I didn't summon anything. I didn't even think about it. I just did it.

I learned what may have been obvious to someone else. Journey died from a brain injury. The impact of him landing on his feet from that distance caused the spinal cord to impale his brain.

The last several pages of the report were from the pathology lab. This is where they take tissue and test it for anything and everything. I learned that when Journey died, he was on *five* prescription medications and one over the counter medication. There were no traces of alcohol, marijuana or other street drugs, only the psychiatric cocktail that his doctor thought would help him.

After a preliminary search and ten minutes on WebMD's site, I learned that Journey was on two different antipsychotic medications, an anti-seizure medication, an antianxiety medication, an antidepressant medication and a hefty dose of Benadryl – often given to induce sleep. According to WebMD, two of the medications interact poorly together. All five of the prescription medications carried warnings about suicide being a common side effect, especially in young adults. Lastly, the concentration levels of one of the antipsychotic medications was 29.4 ng/mL. Printed after that data was the following information: "Therapeutic range, low dose 1-5 ng/mL. Most patients will respond in the range of 5-15 ng/mL; however, some may require higher concentrations to achieve therapeutic effects."

I carefully folded the papers and placed them in their envelope. I put the envelope back in its hiding place in Rex's dresser. I very calmly walked over to our bed and began beating the shit out of the pillows.

I wondered why, when Journey was finally willing

to take the medication, the doctor had given him so many medications and at doses that would be next to impossible to maintain. I wished that the doctor would have recognized that Journey admitting himself to the hospital meant he was willing to take the medication, and therefore given him something manageable.

A few days later, I was visiting with friends. I mentioned that I was thinking of writing that psychiatrist a letter and telling him that Journey had died. I wanted him to know that his treatment hadn't worked at all. One of those friends is a nurse, and I know for certain that she loves me and Journey. With all her heart, she wanted what was best for both of us. She offered a different perspective, "Journey probably presented with all of those symptoms. Of course, his doctor would treat him for them. He did what any psychiatrist would have done." She shrugged and smiled a sad smile and we moved on to a more pleasant subject. I never wrote the letter. I wanted that logic to make sense to me like it did for my friend, but just because a person wants something doesn't always make it so.

Chapter 57

There are two things that come to mind when I recall that first Thanksgiving after Journey's death. One, Journey's name never came up once. The other was that we discovered sun chokes and their profound impact on the digestive system. The sadness of missing Journey and the effects of the sun chokes created quite a juxtaposition; the ache of deep longing and uproarious laughter.

Holidays, of course, are reminders of our loss multiplied. I was dreading the upcoming holiday season and wished I could just go away and come back when it was over.

But we were in town and Josh and Sandy graciously invited us all to their home for dinner and family time. Breaha had read in a cooking magazine about sun chokes, a hearty food like artichokes but meatier and with a nutty flavor. She was delighted to find a vendor at her local farmer's market who had sun chokes by the bushel basket. She bought a couple of pounds of them and made them into a tasty side-dish for our Thanksgiving dinner.

On the way home that night, even though it was a chilly evening, the car windows kept going down and up. Once home and settled around the table with a board game, one after the other, we would excuse ourselves and leave the room for a moment before coming back to the game. Finally, Zach asked if anyone else was experiencing a lot of gas. Laughing, we all agreed that we were. One of us was passing gas every minute or two and a couple of times all of us in stereo. "Anal acoustics!" someone shouted. "Butt bugles!" We all roared.

Breaha called Josh, "Um...well this is a weird question, but are you guys experiencing, well, a lot of gas?" Breaha laughed at something Josh said and hung up. It was indeed a family affair.

Like a bunch of adolescents, we laughed and joked with each other every time someone passed gas. Rex coined the term "one cheek sneaks" and we discussed the merits of silent but deadly bombs over the loud but innocuous ones. All night our uncorked symphony provided comic relief. I thought of Journey's sense of humor and his boyish attitude about "farts." In the middle of a laughing jag, I started to sob. Our game was forgotten, and Rex gathered me into his arms. Seeing me cry triggered Breaha's tears and soon Zach was embracing her.

How could the whole afternoon and evening pass without one mention of Journey? I suppose all of us had our separate thoughts about him throughout the day, felt the loss in our own way, but for whatever reason we never spoke them. Maybe no one wanted to mention his name in case I had forgotten that he died. I say this tongue in cheek of course, but here is something that I know now that I didn't know before. The person who is grieving doesn't forget. The memories, the longing, may not be in the forefront of their mind in any given moment, but it is there nonetheless. It is just under the surface like a low-grade fever. It doesn't matter to me if I am thinking of Journey in that instant or not, I will always welcome his name. His name is like music to me. When people say it, they are remembering him and that his life mattered.

Chapter 58

Christmas was fast approaching, and I was dreading the thought of it as well. I kept thinking "This will be the first Christmas without Journey," but then I realized that wasn't really true. Journey had been with us only one of the past four Christmases. Granted, he was alive then, but he was either in a hospital, a treatment center or simply refused to join us. It was painful to not have him with us those past holidays, but now I saw it as a tiny blessing. We could do this. We had done it before.

When I could step back from my pain and be objective, I saw that in many ways I had more preparation for this than one might think. When Journey was first symptomatic, he spent an entire year believing he was dying of an unknown disease in his gut. He insisted that we talk about the fact that he wouldn't always be alive. He asked me to role play with him what life would be like when he was gone. And although I didn't believe it at the time, I went along with it.

Grief, I have come to understand, is a lot like the weather, unpredictable and unavoidable. A storm may blow in and last for a few minutes or a few days. Likewise, the calm and beautiful mornings remind us of all there is to appreciate.

Gradually, I began to experience more calm. I stopped looking for Journey in the face of every college student I saw. Without trying, I began to see him in the beauty around me.

Occasionally, I catch a whiff of him or feel his love in the warmth of the sun or in a chord of music or someone's laughter. Sometimes, when witnessing something beautiful like a sunset or my grandchildren's faces, I can feel Journey seeing them with me through my eyes. It is a remarkable feeling of connectedness that is difficult to explain and yet is as evident as my own breath. I know with certainty that Journey is everywhere, and that everywhere does indeed include here.

Chapter 59

I am not on a path that was cut short, I'm simply on a short path. Some combination of destiny and free choice mixed up this batch of reality. I hope that after my death, the laws of the universe allow me to witness the rest of humanity. Even if I cannot play the sport, I'm a fan of humanity and I'd like to watch.

~Journey, Summer 2010

Dear Journey,

It has been four years and four months since you transcended your physical body and, admittedly, my faith has taken a beating. I was devastated and shocked when you died. My heart was broken, and I couldn't imagine it ever being whole again. It seemed impossible that I had seen your face or heard your voice for the last time.

In the years leading up to your death, I prayed with a fierceness I had never known before. I searched endlessly for answers and petitioned for miracles. Since I couldn't imagine anything else, I always believed in your full recovery. Naively, I thought that if I prayed enough or loved enough, I could change your course. When you died, it felt like the ultimate betrayal – from you and from God. It has taken a while, but I know now that your course was never mine to change.

In the months following your transition, I witnessed little miracles sprinkled throughout my days. God showed up through countless people to hold me up and love me through my sorrow. God even sent a pigeon to roost in our backyard for a few days to ease my worried heart. I found that if I put my attention on something with an open heart and a true desire, it almost always showed up. I had to admit that my prayers were being answered every day in countless ways.

One of the answered prayers is knowing that our love, yours and mine, didn't die when you did. In fact, in some ways it has intensified. In the most unexpected moments, I feel your presence and your love influencing me.

At first, I worried about your soul. But I don't any more. I know that you are one with God because your love and God's love feel pretty much the same to me. Yours comes with your unique signature and almost always some form of humor. Otherwise, both are vastly profound and consistently present if I quiet myself and tune to the frequency of Love.

I certainly have a greater capacity for compassion. When I see people on the street that look different from me, I look them in the eye and acknowledge them as fellow travelers along an exhilarating and sometimes challenging path. I offer them a smile and a kind word, knowing that regardless of a person's appearance, they have value.

There came a day after you died, when my heart was broken wide open and I understood it was my job to fill that empty, broken-open place with *something*. The question became, "With what? Would I become a bitter person who was defined by sorrow, or would I keep believing in love?" I choose love as often as I am able. I am motivated, Journey, because that is where I feel you.

That love, and my desire to use what I have learned for betterment, has led me to many miraculous things. Most notably, I have met people who have had their own experiences with mental illness and found their way back. I have met doctors and psychiatrists who understand the intersection of the symptoms of mental illness and, of all things, *gut* health!

Some researchers and cutting-edge psychiatrists would say that you, Journey, were at least partially accurate when you insisted that your problems originated in your colon. I cried when I read that some psychiatrists are having great success with their patients by starting there first. I think of how relieved we would have been had we found one of these doctors while you were alive.

I know more than ever that there are pathways to optimal wellness regardless of a person's symptoms. And no one path is right for everyone. I can't help but wonder, though, if it would have made a difference if we had found a single collection of all these resources when you were struggling? What if we had found a place that offered hope as well as a comprehensive list of all possible solutions that were known to restore balance to those touched by mental illness? I am certain I would have felt more optimistic and less alone.

I began to ponder and speculate and daydream. What if there was a place where allopathic, naturopathic, homeopathic, all the "pathics", played well together? A place where evidence-based research and education were valued, and the mission was to provide resources that brought about real change; a place where others found hope, too. I imagined a great big container with everything helpful, hopeful and true within it.

And then, something miraculous happened. I began to meet others with a similar vision. There are doctors, researchers, ministers, therapists, professors, people of all walks of life, who see the possibility of profound change and true recovery from the symptoms of mental illness.

These folks and I agreed to create and nurture a tax-exempt foundation where everyone can experience hope and change. We chose to name this foundation Hattas Shay International (HSI) after two wonderful men. Hattas, after an extraordinary man and visionary that I first met at your memorial. Mark Hattas believes, like us, that there is indeed a path to wellness and optimal living. And the Shay part, well that of course is after you, Journey Shay.

From the inspiration of HSI, sprang a meaningful project that we lovingly call Journey's Dream. Those who know you, know that it was your hope and dream to find answers. You always wanted the best possible outcome for humanity.

It is my deepest desire that anyone struggling with life, addictions or other mental health challenges, as well as their loved ones and families, will find Journey's Dream. This project, named after you, is committed to empowering those touched by mental illness to find hope and resources that promote true wellness and optimal living.

Would knowing what I know now change the outcome of your life and death? I honestly don't know. When I ask, "What if?" I am reminded that you told me the moment you were born, that you would leave before me. Later, as a three-year-old, you had a direct visit from Jesus informing you that you "would have a shiny body like his one day..." Did you, as a soul, know then that your stay here on earth would be brief?

I am beginning to think that perhaps your life *and death* were a part of the same beautiful and complex package.

I have come to accept that I may not have the answers to these questions while I am in a physical body. Sometimes we just have to wait. In the meantime, know that you will always occupy a place in my heart. You have been a profound teacher and continue to be an inspiration to me and many others.

From your limitless view, with God as your witness, please continue to guide and inspire our work.

I will love you forever,

Mom

Epilogue

If you or someone you love is struggling with mental health challenges, find support at www. journeysdream.org. We, at Journey's Dream, believe with comprehensive support, and the proper training and toolset(s), all people can achieve and sustain optimal health and well-being.

Journey's Dream is a resource hub that was born from the desire to have effective solutions available for you and/or your loved ones. It is a portal to a world of mental health solutions including:

- Access to a global network of physicians and practitioners who have supported patients through mental illness to renewed health.
- A collection of resources that have been used to successfully bring about mental wellness.
- Interactive programs proven to facilitate

transformation through the application of simple tools.

- A community of mentors and peers who have experienced optimal health after a mental health challenge(s).

Journey's Dream is continuously growing and evolving as we learn of physicians, practitioners and resources that are in alignment with our vision and mission. If you are seeking resources or wish to collaborate as a practitioner, please visit Journey's Dream at www.journeysdream.org

In Closing

If you enjoyed reading *Journey*, and found its message helpful, would you be so kind as to leave an honest review on my book page at Amazon? Reviews are so important to authors and to potential readers. Even a very short and simple review is greatly appreciated.

Acknowledgements

I would like to thank my children, Joshua, Breaha and Journey. Because of you, I know the gift of all-embracing love and have had the honor of being called "Mom."

To my husband, Rex, who has been my love, friend and companion through life's greatest joys and sorrows, I give my heartfelt thanks and appreciation.

I feel unspeakable love and appreciation for my grandchildren; whose pure joy is a reminder of humanity at its best.

For their encouragement and early mentoring, I would like to thank Breaha Wallin, Stephanie Amada and Jordan Poll. Thank you, Heather Paris and Becky Blanton for your editing skills and expertise.

Someone once told me that the publishing process would take as long as the writing, and they were right. A skilled guide and mentor is a must. To that end, I offer my profound gratitude to Melissa Wilson and Networlding Publishing, Inc. Thank you for believing in my vision.

Benjamin P. Roque (B-Ro) at 99Designs, thank you for the beautiful illustration and cover design.

To the community who held our family in the space of love during Journey's struggles and after his transition, I offer my heartfelt appreciation.

And lastly, to anyone who knew and loved Journey, thank you. Thank you for remembering his love, brilliance, humor and compassion.

Made in the USA
Middletown, DE
01 February 2019